Zaner-Bloser

SPELLING CONNECTIONS

J. Richard Gentry, Ph.D.

2

Series Author
J. Richard Gentry, Ph.D.

Editorial Development: Cottage Communications

Art and Production: PC&F

Photography: George C. Anderson: cover; pages I, 4, 7, 256, 257; SUPERSTOCK ©: p. 12; p. 31; p. 60; p. 61; p. 90; p. 91; p. 102; p. 103; p. 120; p. 162; p. 180; p. 181; p. 192; p. 198; p. 199; p. 211; The Stock Market: p. 13, © 90 William Whitehurst; p. 25, © 98 Tom Stewart; p. 37, © 97 Ariel Skelley; p. 49, © Randy Ury 1992; p. 66, © 97 Peter Steiner; p. 72, © Alan Schein; p. 73, © 94 Zefa Germany; p. 85, © 88 Dave Wilhelm; p. 96, © Roy Morsch; p. 109, © 94 Ed Bock; p. 121 © Michael A. Keller Studios Ltd. 1994; p. 127, © 97 John Scheiber; p. 138, © Tom Stewart 90; p. 205, © 96 Chuck Savage; p. 210, © 87 Ed Bock; Tony Stone Images: p. 18, © Chad Slattery; p. 54, © James Balog; p. 84, © Joe Cornish; p. 108, © Martin Barraud; p. 139, © Peter Cade; p. 144, © John Warden; p. 145, © Peter Cade; p. 156, © Art Wolfe; p. 157, © Renee Lynn; p. 163, © Christopher Arnesen; p. 169, © Gary Vestal; p. 174, © Darryl Torckler; p. 175, © Doug Armand; p. 204, © David Hanover; FPG International: p. 24, © Telegraph Colour Library 1997; p. 30, © 1998 David Fleetham; p. 36, © Dick Luria 1990; p. 48, © Jeffrey Sylvester 1988; p. 55, © Paul Avis 1994; p. 97, © Bruce Byers 1992; p. 132, © Jay Brenner 1987; p. 168, © Bruce Byers 1986; p. 193, © Thomas Lindley 1987; p. 217, © Ron Chapple 1995; Artville ©: p. 67; p. 216, © Burke-Triolo Productions

Illustrations: Laurel Aiello: pages 22, 225, 226, 227, 228, 229, 230, 233, 234, 235, 236, 237, 238, 239, 240, 242, 243, 244, 245, 246, 247, 249, 250, 253; Dave Blanchette: pages 35, 47, 59, 65, 107, 143; Nan Brooks: pages 34, 46, 58, 64, 69, 100, 136; Tom Elliott: pages 19, 77, 126, 133, 179, 191; Rusty Fletcher: pages 160, 165, 173, 196, 207, 214; Collin Fry: pages 83, 94, 118, 124, 155; Kate Gorman: pages 52, 95, 106, 125, 141; Steve Henry: pages 82, 89, 117, 123, 137, 154, 159, 161, 172, 190, 195, 201, 208; Claude Martinot: pages 38, 39, 40, 74, 75, 76, 110, 111, 112, 113, 114, 146, 147, 148, 149, 150, 182, 183, 184, 185, 186, 218, 219, 220, 221, 222; Bill Ogden: pages 9, 10, 16, 17, 21, 23, 28, 29, 53, 71, 87, 88, 101, 119, 129, 130, 134, 142, 166, 167, 178, 189, 197, 202, 203, 209, 215; George Ulrich: pages 11, 131; Vickie Woodworth: pages 51, 57, 70

ISBN: 0-7367-0038-2

Zaner-Bloser, Inc., P.O. Box 16764, Columbus, Ohio 43216-6764 (1-800-421-3018)

Printed in the United States of America   00 01 02 03 BA 5 4 3 2

Contents

Spelling Study Strategy

Look → Say → Cover → See → Write → Check

1 **Look** at the word.

2 **Say** the letters in the word. Think about how each sound is spelled.

3 **Cover** the word with your hand or close your eyes.

4 **See** the word in your mind. Spell the word to yourself.

5 **Write** the word.

6 **Check** your spelling against the spelling in the book.

beginning short a

1. _____

2. _____

middle short a

3. _____

4. _____

5. _____

6. _____

7. _____

8. _____

9. _____

10. _____

Spelling and Thinking

READ THE SPELLING WORDS

1. ask — I **ask** Pat for help.
2. sat — Mom **sat** on the sofa.
3. fan — The **fan** keeps us cool.
4. map — The **map** shows our town.
5. hand — I use my **hand** to wave.
6. cap — Take the **cap** off your head!
7. sad — The bad news made us **sad**.
8. fat — We love our old **fat** dog.
9. bat — I hit the ball with the **bat**.
10. as — Hop and jump **as** I do.

SORT THE SPELLING WORDS

The words on the spelling list have the **short a** sound.

1.–2. Write the words that begin with the **short a** sound.

3.–10. Write the words that have the **short a** sound in the middle.

REMEMBER THE SPELLING STRATEGY

Remember that the **short a** sound in words like **bat** can be spelled **a**.

Spelling ᵃⁿᵈ Phonics

Ending Sounds

1.–3. Write the rhyming words that end with **t**.

Word Structure

Replace the underlined letters to write a spelling word.

4. ca<u>t</u>   5. <u>i</u>s

Rhyming Words

Write a spelling word for each set of clues.

6. Wave this to keep cool. Its name rhymes with **man**.

7. Use this to find your way. Its name rhymes with **tap**.

8. If you feel this way, you are not glad. Its name rhymes with **glad**.

USING THE Dictionary

A dictionary tells you the meanings of words. Write the spelling word for each dictionary meaning.

9. try to find out   10. body part

◆ ◆ ◆

Dictionary Check Check the meaning of your words in your **Spelling Dictionary**.

ask	sat	fan	map	hand
cap	sad	fat	bat	as

Solve the Analogies An analogy compares pairs of words that are connected in some way. For example, you know that socks and mittens are both things to wear. Here is an analogy about things you wear: **Sock** is to **foot** as **mitten** is to **hand**. Write a spelling word to complete each analogy.

1. **Smile** is to **happy** as **frown** is to _____.
2. **Short** is to **tall** as **skinny** is to _____.
3. **Foot** is to **shoe** as **head** is to _____.
4. **Hide** is to **hid** as **sit** is to _____.
5. **Catch** is to **glove** as **hit** is to _____.

Complete the Sentences Write the spelling word to complete each sentence.

6. We can't do this alone. Let's _____ Matt for some help.
7. This is my little sister's glove. It does not fit my _____.
8. How do you get to the zoo? We need a _____ to find the way.
9. We use the _____ on a hot day.
10. The coach showed me how to kick the ball. If I do _____ the coach says, maybe I will score a goal!

Solve the Analogies

1. _____
2. _____
3. _____
4. _____
5. _____

Complete the Sentences

6. _____
7. _____
8. _____
9. _____
10. _____

Spelling and Writing

Proofread a Story

Four words are not spelled correctly in this story.
Write the words correctly.

My Ball Game

I put on my baseball kap. I grab my bit
and glove. I ast my dad to drive me to the
park. He says yes. He is as big a baseball
fen as I am!

Write a Story

Narrative Writing

Write a story for a friend. Tell about something
you did. Be sure to say

- who was there.
- where it happened.
- what happened.

Use as many spelling words as you can.

Proofread Your Writing During ➤

Writing Process

Prewriting
⇩
Drafting
⇩
Revising
⇩
Editing
⇩
Publishing

Proofread your writing for spelling errors as part
of the editing stage in the writing process. Be sure
to check each word carefully. Use a dictionary to
check spelling if you are not sure.

Vocabulary

Strategy Words

Review Words: Short a

Write a word from the box for each clue.

can	dad	man

1. This word is spelled the same forward and backward. It rhymes with **mad**.
2. This word spells the /**k**/ sound with a **c**.
3. girl and boy; woman and _____

Preview Words: Short a

Follow the directions to write each word.

cabin	fancy	hatch

4. fang – g + cy = _____
5. cab + in = _____
6. hat + chip – ip = _____

Connections

Content Words

Social Studies: Building

Write the word from the box that completes each sentence.

tools	hammer	nail	ax

1. You need to use many _____ to build a house.
2. We use a _____ to pound each board into place.
3. We use an _____ to chop some logs for our fire.
4. A _____ will help hold the roof on our new birdhouse.

Apply the Spelling Strategy

Circle the letter that spells the **short a** sound in two of the content words you wrote.

Social Studies: Building

1.

2.

3.

4.

beginning short e

1. _____

middle short e

2. _____

3. _____

4. _____

5. _____

6. _____

7. _____

8. _____

9. _____

10. _____

Spelling and Thinking

READ THE SPELLING WORDS

1.	send	I **send** mail to Dan.
2.	bell	The **bell** rings at noon.
3.	well	We all feel **well** today.
4.	help	Please **help** me carry this bag.
5.	fell	Anna **fell** when she ran.
6.	went	I **went** to the store.
7.	spell	We can **spell** many words.
8.	next	The party is **next** week.
9.	tell	Would you **tell** me a story?
10.	end	How does the story **end**?

SORT THE SPELLING WORDS

The words on the spelling list have the **short e** sound.

1. Write the spelling word that begins with the **short e** sound.

2.–10. Write the spelling words that have the **short e** sound in the middle.

REMEMBER THE SPELLING STRATEGY

Remember that the **short e** sound in words like **bell** can be spelled **e**.

Spelling *and* Phonics

Rhyming Words

Write a spelling word that fits the sentence. The spelling word will rhyme with the underlined word.

1. We _____ into the <u>tent</u>.
2. Did Jim <u>bend</u> the _____ of the straw?

Word Math

Follow the directions to write spelling words.

3. went – nt + ll = _____
4. nest – s + x = _____

Word Structure

Replace the underlined letters to write a spelling word.

5. s<u>a</u>nd   6. sp<u>i</u>ll
7. f<u>a</u>ll   8. b<u>u</u>ll

USING THE Dictionary

Write the spelling word for each dictionary meaning.

9. aid   10. say; talk about

◆ ◆ ◆

Dictionary Check Be sure to check the meaning of your words in your **Spelling Dictionary**.

Rhyming Words

1. _____

2. _____

Word Math

3. _____

4. _____

Word Structure

5. _____

6. _____

7. _____

8. _____

Using the Dictionary

9. _____

10. _____

| send | bell | well | help | fell |
| went | spell | next | tell | end |

Complete the Paragraph

1. _____

2. _____

3. _____

4. _____

5. _____

Complete the Sentences

6. _____

7. _____

8. _____

9. _____

10. _____

Complete the Paragraph Write spelling words to complete the paragraph.

I got a letter from Fred. Fred says he is __1.__. He says he __2.__ to a baseball game last Saturday. His favorite team won the game. He says he will visit me __3.__ week. Fred will come on the train. I will __4.__ Fred a letter soon. I will __5.__ him that I want him to visit.

Complete the Sentences Write a spelling word to complete each sentence.

6. I will _____ you lift the box.
7. I am tired at the _____ of the day.
8. Jen _____ on the ice.
9. Can you _____ the words?
10. We hear the school _____ ring.

Spelling and Writing

Proofread a Paragraph

Four words are not spelled correctly in this paragraph. Write the words correctly.

You Can Help

What if a friend fel and got hurt? Could you help? You could! You could sand someone to get help. You could till an adult. You can't make your friend wel, but you can help.

Proofreading Marks

≡ Make a capital.

/ Make a small letter.

∧ Add something.

℘ Take out something.

⊙ Add a period.

⌗ New paragraph

SP Spelling error

Write a Paragraph

Expository Writing

Tell about a way to help a friend. Write your ideas in a paragraph. Tell
- what could happen.
- what you could do to help.

Use as many spelling words as you can.

Writing Process

Prewriting

⇩

Drafting

⇩

Revising

⇩

Proofread Your Writing During → **Editing**

⇩

Publishing

Proofread your writing for spelling errors as part of the editing stage in the writing process. Be sure to check each word carefully. Use a dictionary to check spelling if you are not sure.

Vocabulary

Strategy Words

Review Words

1. _____

2. _____

3. _____

Preview Words

4. _____

5. _____

6. _____

Review Words: Short e

Write a word from the box for each of these clues.

best	let	pen

1. It rhymes with **met**.
2. It begins like **pot** and ends like **can**.
3. It begins like **boy** and ends like **lost**.

Preview Words: Short e

Write a word from the box for each of these clues.

elephant	lemon	sketch

4. It is a kind of picture.
5. It grows on a tree.
6. It is a big animal.

Connections

Content Words

Math: Operations

Write words from the box to complete the paragraph.

add	ones	sum	tens

We know how to __1.__ numbers with two digits. First, we line up the numbers. This is very important. Then we add the numbers in the __2.__ place. Then we add the numbers in the __3.__ place. This gives us the __4.__. If you follow the steps carefully, your answer will always be correct.

Apply the Spelling Strategy

Circle the letter that spells the **short e** sound in one of the content words you wrote.

Math: Operations

1. _____

2. _____

3. _____

4. _____

$$15 + 32$$

$$- $$

$$47$$

Spelling and Thinking

READ THE SPELLING WORDS

1.	hit	I use a bat to **hit** the ball.
2.	fill	Please **fill** my cup.
3.	will	I **will** eat later.
4.	wind	The **wind** is blowing hard.
5.	miss	I **miss** Ben when he is gone.
6.	milk	A cow gives **milk**.
7.	win	Our team can **win** this game.
8.	hill	He rides a bike up the **hill**.
9.	bill	I pay the **bill** for the meal.
10.	fit	The shoes **fit** me just right.

two consonants the same

1.

2.

3.

4.

5.

two consonants different

6.

7.

one consonant

8.

9.

10.

SORT THE SPELLING WORDS

The words on the spelling list have the **short i** sound.

1.–5. Write the spelling words that end with two consonants that are the same.

6.–7. Write the spelling words that end with two consonants that are different.

8.–10. Write the spelling words that end with one consonant.

REMEMBER THE SPELLING STRATEGY

Remember that the **short i** sound in words like **hill** can be spelled **i**.

Spelling ^{and} Phonics

Rhyming Words

Write a spelling word that fits the sentence. The spelling word will rhyme with the underlined word.

1. There is <u>still</u> time to run up that _____.
2. <u>Jill</u> _____ help us dig this hole.
3. Keep your <u>chin</u> up. We can _____ this game!
4. Use your <u>mitt</u> to catch the ball she _____.

Word Structure

5. Change the first letter in **silk** to make this spelling word.
6. Change one letter in **wand** to make this spelling word.
7. Change the last letter in **film** to make this spelling word.

USING THE Dictionary

The words in a dictionary are in a-b-c order.

8.–10. Write these words in a-b-c order.

    fit   bill   miss

◆ ◆ ◆

Dictionary Check Be sure to check the a-b-c order of the words in your **Spelling Dictionary**.

Rhyming Words

1. _____

2. _____

3. _____

4. _____

Word Structure

5. _____

6. _____

7. _____

Using the Dictionary

8. _____

9. _____

10. _____

Spelling and Reading

hit	fill	will	wind	miss
milk	win	hill	bill	fit

Complete the Sentences Write a spelling word to complete each sentence.

1. Do the clothes _____ you?
2. Sarah _____ the ball.
3. Jerry _____ visit soon.
4. Do you _____ your lost cat?

Solve the Analogies An analogy compares pairs of words that are connected in some way. For example, you know that a kitten and a puppy are both baby animals. Here is an analogy about animals: **Kitten** is to **cat** as **puppy** is to **dog**. Write a spelling word to complete each analogy.

5. **Open** is to **close** as **lose** is to _____.
6. **Suitcase** is to **pack** as **glass** is to _____.
7. **Lake** is to **pond** as **mountain** is to _____.
8. **Dime** is to **coin** as **dollar** is to _____.

Complete the Groups Write the spelling word that belongs in each group.

9. rain, snow, _____
10. water, juice, _____

Complete the Sentences

1.
2.
3.
4.

Solve the Analogies

5.
6.
7.
8.

Complete the Groups

9.
10.

22

Spelling and Writing

Proofread a Poster

Four words are not spelled correctly on this poster. Write the words correctly.

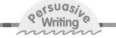 Grant School Baseball Game

What: Teachers Against Kids

Where: Grant Park

When: May 15 at 10 a.m.

Come to the hil. This well be a great game. Watch the best team winn! Don't mis it! This game is sure to be a hit!

Proofreading Marks

≡ Make a capital.

/ Make a small letter.

∧ Add something.

℮ Take out something.

⊙ Add a period.

⌗ New paragraph

SP Spelling error

Write a Poster

Persuasive Writing

Write a poster for an event. Be sure to tell
- what the event is.
- where and when it will take place.
- why people should come.

Use as many spelling words as you can.

Proofread Your Writing During

Proofread your writing for spelling errors as part of the editing stage in the writing process. Be sure to check each word carefully. Use a dictionary to check spelling if you are not sure.

Writing Process

Prewriting

⬇

Drafting

⬇

Revising

⬇

Editing

⬇

Publishing

Vocabulary

Strategy Words

Review Words

1. _____
2. _____
3. _____

Preview Words

4. _____
5. _____
6. _____

Review Words: Short i

Write the word from the box for each clue.

big	bit	spin

1. It begins like **spell** and ends like **win**.
2. It rhymes with **pit**.
3. hot and cold, little and _____

Preview Words: Short i

Add the missing letters to write words from the box.

fish	kitten	little

4. f __ s __
5. l __ t __ le
6. k __ tt __ n

Connections

Content Words

Science: Temperature

Write the word from the box that completes each sentence.

| frost | thaw | chill | melt |

1. Take the food out of the freezer so it will _____.
2. The ice on the pond will not _____ on a cold day like today.
3. I need a jacket because of the _____ in the air.
4. On cold mornings, there is _____ on the window.

Apply the Spelling Strategy

Circle the letter that spells the **short i** sound in one of the content words you wrote.

Science: Temperature

1. _____

2. _____

3. _____

4. _____

three letters

1. _____

2. _____

3. _____

4. _____

5. _____

6. _____

four letters

7. _____

8. _____

9. _____

10. _____

Spelling and Thinking

READ THE SPELLING WORDS

1.	dog	The **dog** likes its bone.
2.	doll	I play with a **doll**.
3.	stop	We **stop** at the red light.
4.	cot	You can sleep on a **cot**.
5.	log	This **log** is from that tree.
6.	fog	We cannot see in the **fog**.
7.	spot	The dog has one black **spot**.
8.	pond	Fish live in the **pond**.
9.	nod	I **nod** when I mean yes.
10.	lot	Two cups is a **lot** of milk!

SORT THE SPELLING WORDS

1.–6. Write the three-letter spelling words that have the **short o** sound.

7.–10. Write the four-letter spelling words that have the **short o** sound.

REMEMBER THE SPELLING STRATEGY

Remember that the **short o** sound in words like **cot** can be spelled **o**.

Spelling and Phonics

Rhyming Words

Write a spelling word for each set of clues.

1. You can sleep on it. Its name rhymes with **not**.
2. It is a piece of a tree. Its name rhymes with **frog**.
3. It is a mark. Its name rhymes with **hot**.
4. It is like a cloud. Its name rhymes with **hog**.

Word Structure

5. Change the vowel in **step** to make this spelling word.
6. Change the last two letters in **post** to make this spelling word.
7. Change the first two letters in **call** to make this spelling word.

USING THE Dictionary

The words in a dictionary are in a-b-c order.

8.–10. Write these words in a-b-c order.

nod   dog   lot

◆ ◆ ◆

Dictionary Check Be sure to check the a-b-c order of the words in your **Spelling Dictionary**.

Spelling and Reading

dog	doll	stop	cot	log
fog	spot	pond	nod	lot

Use the Clues

1. _____

2. _____

3. _____

Complete the Paragraph

4. _____

5. _____

6. _____

7. _____

8. _____

9. _____

10. _____

Use the Clues Write the spelling word that fits each clue.

1. You can do this to say yes.
2. You can be in this, but you can't see in it.
3. You can burn this in a fire.

Complete the Paragraph Write spelling words to complete the paragraph.

My Pet

I have a pet __4.__. He is mostly brown, but he has one black __5.__. On nice days, we like to play in the yard. He is a __6.__ of fun. The only trouble is he likes to hide my toy __7.__. One day he hid her under a __8.__ we keep in the bedroom. Another time, he dropped her in the little __9.__ behind our house. My doll got all wet! I had to hang her on a line to dry. How can I make that dog of mine __10.__ hiding my doll?

28

Spelling and Writing

Proofread a Paragraph

Four words are not spelled correctly in this paragraph. Write the words correctly.

By the Water

There is a pand near my house. My doag Spot and I sit there. We can see small fish. We can hear birds. A lat of insects fly by. Sometimes a big, green frog sits on a loag.

     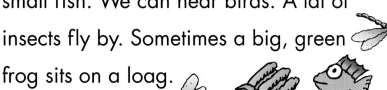

Proofreading Marks

⫤ Make a capital.

/ Make a small letter.

∧ Add something.

℘ Take out something.

⊙ Add a period.

⌗ New paragraph

(SP) Spelling error

Write a Paragraph

Descriptive Writing

Write a paragraph about a place where you like to sit. Tell

- what you see there.
- what you hear, smell, or touch there.
- what you do there.

Use as many spelling words as you can.

Writing Process

Prewriting
⇩
Drafting
⇩
Revising
⇩
Editing
⇩
Publishing

Proofread Your Writing During ▶ **Editing**

Proofread your writing for spelling errors as part of the editing stage in the writing process. Be sure to check each word carefully. Use a dictionary to check spelling if you are not sure.

Vocabulary

Strategy Words

Review Words

1. _____

2. _____

3. _____

Preview Words

4. _____

5. _____

6. _____

Review Words: Short o

Write a word from the box for each clue.

body	got	mom

1. sit, sat; get, _____
2. This word has two syllables.
3. father and mother, dad and _____

Preview Words: Short o

Write a word from the box for each clue.

block	octopus	popcorn

4. This word contains two smaller words.

5. This word has three syllables.

6. This word begins like **blow** and ends like **clock**.

Connections

Content Words

Social Studies: Careers

Write the word from the box that fits each sentence.

| doctor | nurse | dentist | helpers |

1. The _____ helps the doctor during my checkup.
2. The _____ looks at my teeth and says I have no cavities!
3. The class _____ do jobs for the teacher each week.
4. You should see a _____ when you are sick.

Apply the Spelling Strategy

Circle the letter that spells the **short o** sound in one of the content words you wrote.

Social Studies: Careers

1. _____
2. _____
3. _____
4. _____

three letters

1. _____

2. _____

3. _____

4. _____

four letters

5. _____

6. _____

7. _____

8. _____

9. _____

10. _____

Spelling and Thinking

READ THE SPELLING WORDS

1. jug   The **jug** has water in it.
2. mud   Rain turns dirt to **mud**.
3. just   I have **just** one cat.
4. hunt   I **hunt** for my missing glasses.
5. club   Tina will join our **club**.
6. drum   Sam plays the **drum** well.
7. jump   I can **jump** two feet.
8. dust   Juan will **dust** the old table.
9. rub   I **rub** the cat's back.
10. cup   Ann drinks a **cup** of milk.

SORT THE SPELLING WORDS

The words on the spelling list have the **short u** sound.

1.–4. Write the three-letter spelling words that have the **short u** sound.

5.–10. Write the four-letter spelling words that have the **short u** sound.

REMEMBER THE SPELLING STRATEGY

Remember that the **short u** sound in words like **cup** can be spelled **u**.

Spelling and Phonics

Rhyming Words ━━━━━━━━━━━━━━━━

1.–2. Write the words that rhyme with **must**.

3.–4. Write the words that rhyme with **tub**.

Sounds and Letters ━━━━━━━━━━━━

5. Write the word that ends with the same two letters as **lamp**.

6. Write the word that ends with the same two letters as **pup**.

7. Write the word that ends with the same two letters as **plum**.

Word Structure ━━━━━━━━━━━━━━

Replace the underlined letters to write a spelling word.

8. <u>h</u>ug   **9.** h<u>i</u>nt

USING THE Dictionary

A dictionary tells you the meanings of words. Write the spelling word for this dictionary meaning.

10. soft, wet dirt

◆ ◆ ◆

Dictionary Check Be sure to check the meaning of the word in your **Spelling Dictionary**.

Rhyming Words

1.

2.

3.

4.

Sounds and Letters

5.

6.

7.

Word Structure

8.

9.

Using the Dictionary

10.

jug	mud	just	hunt	club
drum	jump	dust	rub	cup

Replace the Words

Replace the Words Write the spelling word that could best take the place of each underlined word or words.

1. Pam will <u>leap</u> over the fence.
2. We <u>look hard</u> for the missing cat.
3. That baby is <u>only</u> six months old.
4. We like to play in the <u>wet dirt</u>.

Solve the Analogies

Solve the Analogies Write a spelling word to complete each comparison.

5. **Food** is to **plate** as **milk** is to _____.
6. **Blow** is to **horn** as **beat** is to _____.

Complete the Sentences

Complete the Sentences Write the spelling word to complete each sentence.

7. The water is in that big _____.
8. My cat likes to _____ its back on the side of that tree.
9. Our _____ meets in the tree house.
10. We _____ that shelf every week.

Replace the Words

1.
2.
3.
4.

Solve the Analogies

5.
6.

Complete the Sentences

7.
8.
9.
10.

Spelling and Writing

Proofread a Letter

Four words are not spelled correctly in this letter. Write the words correctly.

> Dear Grandma,
>
> We jist got home from Fun Time Park. We went on the tiger hnut ride. We made a mess in the mudd room. We played games in the kids' clob. We even went on the sky jump ride. It was so much fun!
>
> Love,
>
> Meg

Proofreading Marks

☰	Make a capital.
/	Make a small letter.
∧	Add something.
ℓ	Take out something.
⊙	Add a period.
⌗	New paragraph
SP	Spelling error

Write a Letter

Narrative Writing

Write a letter to an adult. Tell about a special day. Be sure to tell

- where you went.
- what you did.

Use as many spelling words as you can.

Proofread Your Writing During ➤

Writing Process

Prewriting
⇩
Drafting
⇩
Revising
⇩
Editing
⇩
Publishing

Proofread your writing for spelling errors as part of the editing stage in the writing process. Be sure to check each word carefully. Use a dictionary to check spelling if you are not sure.

Vocabulary

Review Words

1. _____

2. _____

3. _____

Preview Words

4. _____

5. _____

6. _____

Review Words: Short u

Write a word from the box for each clue.

bump	must	rug

1. It begins like **big**. It rhymes with **jump** and **dump**.

2. It begins like **room**. It rhymes with **tug** and **bug**.

3. It begins like **mom**. It rhymes with **dust** and **just**.

Preview Words: Short u

Decide which letters are missing. Write a word from the box.

until	sunny	ugly

4. u __ t __ l

5. u __ l __

6. s __ nn __

Connections

Content Words

Math: Operations

Write the word from the box that fits each definition.

number	match	count	group

1. You do this when you put numbers or things in sets.
2. You do this when you say numbers in order.
3. This can be 1, 2, or 3.
4. You do this when you put together a set and the number that names the set.

Apply the Spelling Strategy

Circle the letter that spells the **short u** sound in one of the content words you wrote.

Math: Operations

1. _____

2. _____

3. _____

4. _____

Assessment and Review

Assessment Units 1–5

Each Assessment Word in the box fits one of the spelling strategies you have studied over the past five weeks. Read the spelling strategies. Then write each Assessment Word under the unit number it fits.

Unit 1
1.–2. The **short a** sound in words like **bat** can be spelled **a**.

Unit 2
3.–4. The **short e** sound in words like **bell** can be spelled **e**.

Unit 3
5.–6. The **short i** sound in words like **hill** can be spelled **i**.

Unit 4
7.–8. The **short o** sound in words like **cot** can be spelled **o**.

Unit 5
9.–10. The **short u** sound in words like **cup** can be spelled **u**.

fond
belt
silk
moss
nap
yell
spun
gill
mad
mug

Unit 1

1. _____
2. _____

Unit 2

3. _____
4. _____

Unit 3

5. _____
6. _____

Unit 4

7. _____
8. _____

Unit 5

9. _____
10. _____

Review Unit 1: Short a

ask	map	fan	hand	as

Write a spelling word to complete each sentence. The spelling word will rhyme with the underlined word.

1. May I _____ what's on your <u>mask</u>?
2. Put your _____ in the <u>sand</u>.
3. John <u>has</u> the same name _____ his dad.
4. Heidi <u>ran</u> to get the _____.
5. Hold the _____ in your <u>lap</u>.

Review Unit 2: Short e

tell	send	next	went	well

Write the spelling word that rhymes with each word or group of words.

6. spend, lend, bend
7. bent, dent, rent
8. text

Write the spelling word that fits each shape.

9. ⌐⊔⌐

10. ⌐⊔⌐

1. _____

2. _____

3. _____

4. _____

5. _____

6. _____

7. _____

8. _____

9. _____

10. _____

Review Unit 3: Short i

will	milk	miss	wind	hit

Write the spelling word that completes each sentence.

1. If you help me, I _____ help you.

2. How far can you _____ the ball?

3. When will it be summer? I really _____ being able to swim.

4. Is there enough _____ outside to fly a kite today?

5. Sue drank two glasses of _____ with her dinner tonight.

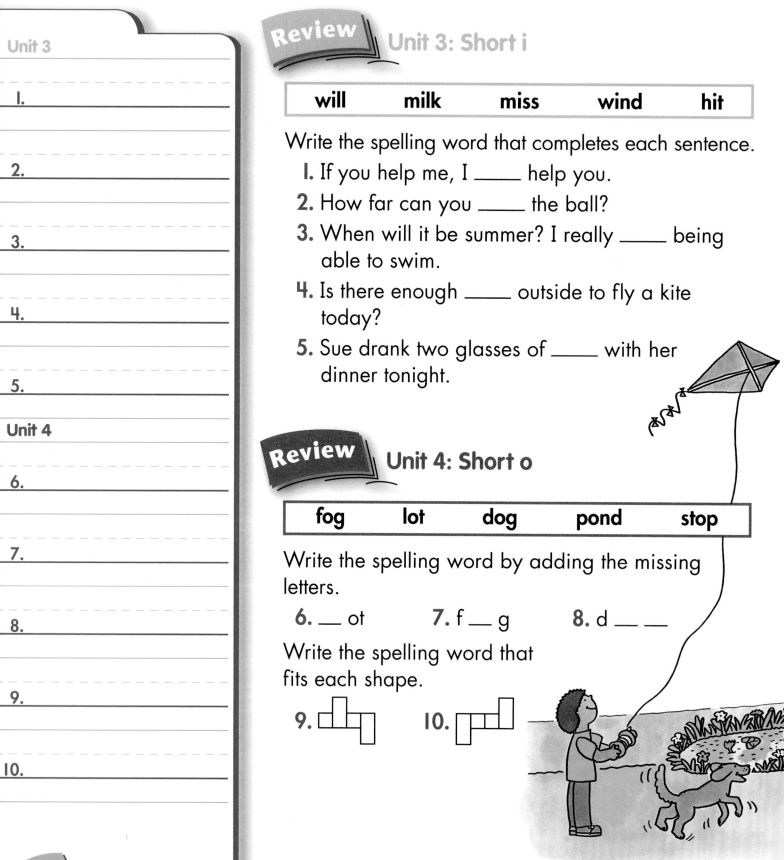

Review Unit 4: Short o

fog	lot	dog	pond	stop

Write the spelling word by adding the missing letters.

6. __ ot   7. f __ g   8. d __ __

Write the spelling word that fits each shape.

9. [grid shape]   10. [grid shape]

cup	jump	mud	just	dust

Change one letter in each underlined word to write a spelling word.

1. The wind brought a lot of <u>rust</u>.
2. I have <u>must</u> enough pencils.
3. That dirty dog must have been in a <u>mad</u> puddle.
4. How high can you <u>lump</u>?
5. You may drink from this <u>cap</u>.

GAME **Spelling Study Strategy**

Spelling Tic-Tac-Toe

Practicing spelling words can be fun if you make it into a game. Here's an idea you can try with a friend.

1. Write your spelling words in a list. Ask your friend to do the same. Trade spelling lists.

2. Draw a tic-tac-toe board on a piece of paper. Decide who will use **X** and who will use **O**.

3. Ask your partner to call out the first word on your list. Spell it out loud. If you spell it correctly, make an **X** or an **O** (whichever you are using) on the tic-tac-toe board. If you misspell a word, you lose your turn.

4. Take turns until you have practiced all the words in your list or won the game.

Unit 5

1. _____

2. _____

3. _____

4. _____

5. _____

Grammar, Usage, and Mechanics

What Is a Sentence?

A sentence tells one complete thought. It begins with a capital letter and ends with an end mark. A sentence has two parts.

The subject tells what the sentence is about:

The bus came late.

The predicate tells what happened:

The bus **came late**.

A. Is each group of words a sentence? Write **yes** or **no**.

    1. went to the store   **2.** I will get milk.

    3. You need a bun.   **4.** A big ham

    5. The dog cannot come in.

B. Complete each sentence with a word from the box. Begin each sentence with a capital letter.

milk	jump	fog

    6. _____ looks like clouds.

    7. _____ tastes good.

    8. Both frogs _____.

A.

1. _____

2. _____

3. _____

4. _____

5. _____

B.

6. _____

7. _____

8. _____

Proofreading Strategy

Check Each Sentence

Good writers always proofread their writing for spelling mistakes. Here is a strategy you can use to proofread your papers.

Look at the first word in each sentence. Make sure that it starts with a capital letter. Look at each word one at a time and check its spelling. Then look at the last word in each sentence. Make sure that it is followed by an end mark.

Electronic Spelling

File Naming

A word processor can make writing fun. You can add pictures and fancy type. You can create work that you want to keep, such as stories and reports.

You will often save your work. To do this, you must name the computer file. If you misspell the file name, you may not be able to find your work later.

Four file names have a misspelled word. Write the misspelled word correctly. Write **OK** for the others.

1. Things to Ask About
2. Town Mapp
3. Letters to Sende
4. A dag story
5. A Lot of Old Things
6. The Nexck Homework

Electronic Spelling

1. _____

2. _____

3. _____

4. _____

5. _____

6. _____

Spelling and Thinking

READ THE SPELLING WORDS

1.	chalk	I use **chalk** to write.
2.	fall	Winter comes after **fall**.
3.	wall	I cannot see over that **wall**.
4.	talk	We **talk** on the phone.
5.	ball	Throw me the **ball**.
6.	walk	Let's **walk** to the store.
7.	small	A frog is a **small** animal.
8.	tall	Matt is six feet **tall**.
9.	call	Did you **call** my name?
10.	all	I drank **all** my milk.

end in ll

1. _____

2. _____

3. _____

4. _____

5. _____

6. _____

7. _____

end in lk

8. _____

9. _____

10. _____

SORT THE SPELLING WORDS

The words on the spelling list have the vowel sound in **ball**.

1.–7. Write the spelling words that have the vowel sound in **ball** and end with **ll**.

8.–10. Write the spelling words that have the vowel sound in **ball** and end with **lk**.

REMEMBER THE SPELLING STRATEGY

Remember the vowel sound you hear in **ball** and **talk** can be spelled **a**.

Spelling ᵃⁿᵈ Phonics

Word Structure

Change the underlined letter to make a spelling word.

1. w<u>e</u>ll
2. cal<u>m</u>
3. ba<u>i</u>l

Sound and Letter Patterns

4. Write the spelling word that has three letters and ends with a double consonant.

5.–6. Now add letters to your answer to number 4 to make two rhyming words that have four letters.

7. Now add two letters to your answer to number 4 to make a rhyming word with five letters.

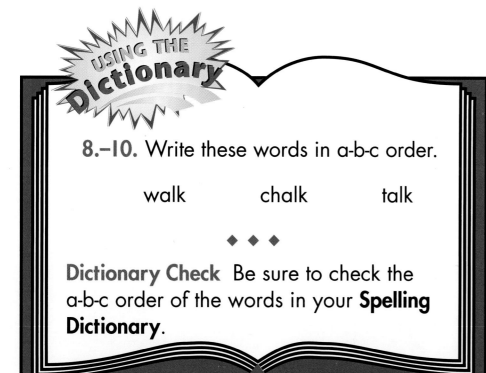

USING THE Dictionary

8.–10. Write these words in a-b-c order.

walk   chalk   talk

◆ ◆ ◆

Dictionary Check Be sure to check the a-b-c order of the words in your **Spelling Dictionary**.

Word Structure

1.
2.
3.

Sound and Letter Patterns

4.
5.
6.
7.

Using the Dictionary

8.
9.
10.

45

Spelling and Reading

chalk	fall	wall	talk	ball
walk	small	tall	call	all

Solve the Analogies

1.

2.

3.

4.

5.

Complete the Word Groups

6.

7.

8.

Complete the Sentences

9.

10.

Solve the Analogies Write a spelling word to complete each analogy.

1. **March** is to **September** as **spring** is to _____.
2. **Empty** is to **full** as **none** is to _____.
3. **Elephant** is to **big** as **mouse** is to _____.
4. **Big** is to **large** as **high** is to _____.
5. **Paper** is to **pen** as **chalkboard** is to _____.

Complete the Word Groups Write the spelling word to complete each group.

6. say, speak, _____
7. run, jog, _____
8. bat, glove, _____

Complete the Sentences Write the spelling word that completes each sentence.

9. We line up along the _____.
10. The nurse will _____ your name.

Spelling and Writing

Proofread a Paragraph

Four words are not spelled correctly in this paragraph. Write the words correctly.

Proofreading Marks

≡ Make a capital.

/ Make a small letter.

∧ Add something.

ℓ Take out something.

⊙ Add a period.

⌗ New paragraph

ⓢⓟ Spelling error

Jones Field

We play ball at Jones Field. It is a short wolk from my house. It is a smoll field, but the grass is nice. My friends al like to play there. Some can even hit the ball over the Jones Field wol.

Write a Paragraph

Descriptive Writing

Write about a place where you like to play. Tell
- where it is.
- what you do there.
- what makes it special.

Use as many spelling words as you can.

Writing Process

Prewriting

⇩

Drafting

⇩

Revising

⇩

Proofread Your Writing During → Editing

⇩

Publishing

Proofread your writing for spelling errors as part of the editing stage in the writing process. Be sure to check each word carefully. Use a dictionary to check spelling if you are not sure.

Vocabulary

Strategy Words

Review Words

1. _____

2. _____

3. _____

Preview Words

4. _____

5. _____

6. _____

Review Words: Vowel Sound in ball

Write a word from the box for each clue.

am	bad	fast

1. It begins like **ball,** but it has a different vowel sound and ending.

2. It does not have the vowel sound in **wall**. It begins with a **short a** sound.

3. It ends like **last**. It begins like **fall**. It has a **short a** sound.

Preview Words: Vowel Sound in ball

Follow the directions to write words from the box.

almost	crawl	crosswalk

4. cross + walk = _____

5. all – l + most = _____

6. crash – ash + awl = _____

Connections

Content Words

Science: Young Animals

Write words from the box to complete the paragraph.

baby	foal	fawn	piglet

Young animals have special names. A young cat is called a kitten. A young dog is called a pup. A young pig is called a __1.__. A young horse is called a __2.__. A young deer is called a __3.__. A young human is called a __4.__.

Apply the Spelling Strategy

Circle the content word you wrote in which the vowel sound is spelled **aw**.

Science: Young Animals

1. _____

2. _____

3. _____

4. _____

49

Spelling and Thinking

dr, fr, br, gr

1.

2.

3.

4.

fl, gl, pl, cl

5.

6.

7.

8.

9.

10.

READ THE SPELLING WORDS

1.	flat	I made a **flat** pancake.
2.	glass	I fill the **glass** with milk.
3.	plant	The **plant** grows in a pot.
4.	dress	Amy wears a red **dress**.
5.	front	Sit in the **front** seat.
6.	bring	May I **bring** you some food?
7.	grass	She cuts the **grass**.
8.	glad	I feel **glad** to be here.
9.	clap	We **clap** to the beat.
10.	class	Our **class** has ten boys in it.

SORT THE SPELLING WORDS

1.–4. Write the spelling words that begin with **dr, fr, br,** or **gr**.

5.–10. Write the spelling words that begin with **fl, gl, pl,** or **cl**.

REMEMBER THE SPELLING STRATEGY

Remember that a **consonant cluster** is two or more consonants together that make more than one sound: **gl** in **glad** and **dr** in **dress**.

Spelling ^{and} Phonics

Rhyming Words

Write a spelling word that fits the sentence. The spelling word will rhyme with the underlined word.

1. An <u>ant</u> was on a leaf of the _____.
2. I frown when I am <u>mad</u>. I smile when I am _____.
3. I will <u>sing</u> for you. Please _____ me the music.
4. He ran for a <u>pass</u> on the green _____.
5. <u>Tap</u> your feet and _____ your hands.

Consonant Clusters

Write the spelling word that begins with the same consonant cluster as the words in each group.

6. from, frog, _____   7. drop, drive, _____

The words in a dictionary are in a-b-c order.

8.–10. Write these words in a-b-c order.

  glass   class   flat

♦ ♦ ♦

Dictionary Check Be sure to check the a-b-c order of the words in your **Spelling Dictionary**.

Rhyming Words

1. _____
2. _____
3. _____
4. _____
5. _____

Consonant Clusters

6. _____
7. _____

Using the Dictionary

8. _____
9. _____
10. _____

51

flat	glass	plant	dress	front
bring	grass	glad	clap	class

Complete the Story Write the spelling words that complete the story.

Dad mowed the ___1.___ in our yard. Then he said, "Let's put some flowers in ___2.___ of our house. They will add many pretty colors to the yard. Will you help me ___3.___ them? You will need to dig some holes. It will be hard work."

I was ___4.___ to help, so I said, "Yes! Let's begin."

"In that case," Dad said, "___5.___ me some tools."

Complete the Sentences Write the spelling word to complete each sentence.

6. We will _____ at the end of the play.

7. Liz will wear a _____ to the party.

8. I showed the picture to my teacher and the _____.

Match the Shape Write the spelling word that matches each shape.

9. 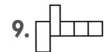   10.

Complete the Story

1. _____
2. _____
3. _____
4. _____
5. _____

Complete the Sentences

6. _____
7. _____
8. _____

Match the Shape

9. _____
10. _____

Spelling AND Writing

Proofread an E-Mail Message

Four words are not spelled correctly in this e-mail message. Write the words correctly.

From: JG99@kids.com
To: Patti@fastmail.com

Patti,

    The school cleanup is on Friday. We will cut the gras in fornt and pick up glass. Dess in old clothes and birng trash bags.

José

Proofreading Marks

≡ Make a capital.

/ Make a small letter.

∧ Add something.

℘ Take out something.

⊙ Add a period.

⌗ New paragraph

SP Spelling error

Write an E-Mail Message

Expository Writing

Write to a friend. Ask him or her to do something with you. Be sure to tell

- the time.
- the place.
- what to bring.

Use as many spelling words as you can.

Writing Process

Prewriting
⇩
Drafting
⇩
Revising
⇩
Proofread Your Writing During ➤ **Editing**
⇩
Publishing

Proofread your writing for spelling errors as part of the editing stage in the writing process. Be sure to check each word carefully. Use a dictionary to check spelling if you are not sure.

Vocabulary

Strategy Words

Review Words

1. _____

2. _____

3. _____

Preview Words

4. _____

5. _____

6. _____

Review Words: Consonant Clusters

Write a word from the box to complete each analogy.

broom	cluck	frog

1. **Hole** is to **snake** as **lily pad** is to _____.
2. **Dig** is to **shovel** as **sweep** is to _____.
3. **Bird** is to **chirp** as **hen** is to _____.

Preview Words: Consonant Clusters

Write a word from the box for each clue.

cliff	grand	platter

4. This word means "a large plate."

5. This word means "great."

6. This is a high place.

Connections

Content Words

Science: Ocean Life

Write the word from the box that fits each set of clues.

| lobster | crab | clam | shrimp |

1. This is a sea animal like a crab. It is caught in a trap.
2. This is an animal with five pairs of legs. It can walk sideways on sand.
3. This is a sea animal with a hard shell that has two parts.
4. This is a small saltwater animal. This word can mean one or more than one.

Apply the Spelling Strategy

Circle the two content words you wrote that begin with a **consonant cluster** with **r** or **l**.

Science: Ocean Life

1. _____
2. _____
3. _____
4. _____

nk

1. _____

2. _____

3. _____

4. _____

ng

5. _____

6. _____

7. _____

8. _____

9. _____

10. _____

Spelling and Thinking

READ THE SPELLING WORDS

1.	wink	Can you **wink** at me?
2.	sing	We **sing** songs in class.
3.	sink	Do not let the boat **sink**.
4.	king	A **king** may wear a crown.
5.	long	That dog has a **long** tail.
6.	ring	The **ring** is made of gold.
7.	hang	I **hang** the shirt on the line.
8.	bank	We get money at the **bank**.
9.	wing	The bird's **wing** is broken.
10.	drink	I **drink** a lot of water.

SORT THE SPELLING WORDS

1.–4. Write the spelling words that end with the consonant cluster **nk**.

5.–10. Write the spelling words that end with the consonant digraph **ng**.

REMEMBER THE SPELLING STRATEGY

Remember that a **consonant cluster** is two or more consonants together that make more than one sound: **nk** in **bank**. A **consonant digraph** is two or more consonants together that make one new sound: **ng** in **ring**.

Spelling ᴬⁿᵈ Phonics

Rhyming Words
Write a spelling word that fits the sentence. The spelling word will rhyme with the underlined word.

1. It is <u>spring</u>! I heard a bird flap its _____.
2. Please <u>bring</u> the _____ his crown.
3. Bees <u>sting</u> and birds _____ pretty songs.
4. The gold <u>thing</u> on her finger is a _____.

Word Structure
Follow the directions to write spelling words.

5. Change one letter in **drank** to make this word.
6. Change one letter in **hand** to make this word.
7. Change two letters in **ball** to make this word.
8. Change two letters in **lost** to make this word.

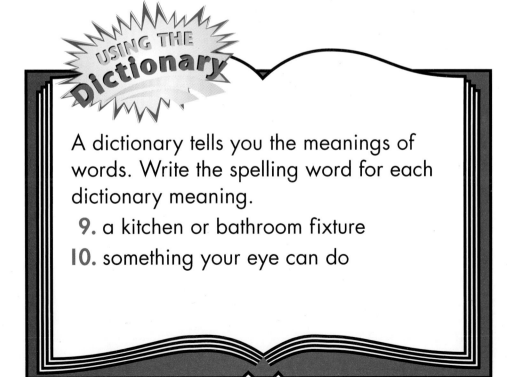

USING THE Dictionary

A dictionary tells you the meanings of words. Write the spelling word for each dictionary meaning.

9. a kitchen or bathroom fixture
10. something your eye can do

Rhyming Words
1.

2.

3.

4.

Word Structure

5.

6.

7.

8.

Using the Dictionary

9.

10.

Spelling and Reading

wink	sing	sink	king	long
ring	hang	bank	wing	drink

Replace the Words Write the spelling word that could best take the place of the underlined word or words.

1. A boat with a hole in it can <u>go down below the water</u>.

2. The <u>person who rules</u> has a lot of power.

3. Mike draws a <u>circle</u> around the right word.

Match the Shape Write the spelling word that completes the sentence and matches the shape.

4. We had to wait in line for a very _____ time.

5. Chang ate a drumstick, and Sam ate a _____ .

Complete the Sentences Write a spelling word to complete each sentence.

6. Jill and I can _____ that song.

7. We _____ the wash outside to dry.

8. Did you just _____ at me?

9. That milk is too hot to _____.

10. I got a roll of dimes at the _____.

Replace the Words

1. _____

2. _____

3. _____

Match the Shape

4. _____

5. _____

Complete the Sentences

6. _____

7. _____

8. _____

9. _____

10. _____

58

Spelling ᴬⁿᵈ Writing

Proofread an Ad

Four words are not spelled correctly in this ad.
Write the words correctly.

RENT MY ROWBOAT JUST $5 A DAY!

It is 10 feet long and will not singk.

It is on the baank of the Haley River.

You can row in it and fish and snig!

You will feel great. You will feel like a keeng.

Call Em at 555-2440.

Proofreading Marks

≡ Make a capital.

/ Make a small letter.

∧ Add something.

℮ Take out something.

⊙ Add a period.

⌗ New paragraph

SP Spelling error

Write an Ad — Persuasive Writing

Write an ad for something you might sell or rent.
Be sure to tell

- what is great about it.
- what it costs.
- how and where to get it.

Use as many spelling words as you can.

Writing Process

Prewriting
⇩
Drafting
⇩
Revising
⇩
Editing
⇩
Publishing

Proofread Your Writing During ➤ Editing

Proofread your writing for spelling errors as part
of the editing stage in the writing process. Be
sure to check each word carefully. Use a
dictionary to check spelling if you are not sure.

Vocabulary

Strategy Words

Review Words

I. _____

2. _____

3. _____

Preview Words

4. _____

5. _____

6. _____

Review Words: nk, ng

Write a word from the box for each of these clues.

bending	doing	going

1. talk, talking; do, _____
2. Add a letter to the beginning of **ending** to make this word.
3. It is the opposite of **stopping**.

Preview Words: nk, ng

Write words from the box by adding the missing letters.

belong	kingdom	think

4. ki __ gd __ m
5. b __ l __ n __
6. th __ n __

Connections

Content Words

Language Arts: Past Tense Verbs

Write the word from the box that fits each clue.

drank	sank	hung	rang

1. This word is the opposite of **floated**.
2. This word rhymes with **hang**. It tells what a phone or a bell did.
3. This word rhymes with **thank**. It is often used with **ate**.
4. If you put **up** after this word, it tells what someone did at the end of a phone call.

Apply the Spelling Strategy

Circle the consonant cluster **nk** in two of the content words you wrote. Underline the consonant digraph **ng** in the other two content words you wrote.

Language Arts:
Past Tense Verbs

1.

2.

3.

4.

61

Spelling and Thinking

short a

1. _____

short e

2. _____

3. _____

short i

4. _____

5. _____

6. _____

short u

7. _____

8. _____

9. _____

10. _____

READ THE SPELLING WORDS

1. give — I **give** the pen to Emma.
2. come — Can you **come** out to play?
3. does — What **does** that robot do?
4. done — He has **done** well in school.
5. been — Have you **been** to the park?
6. head — Take that hat off your **head**.
7. some — We stopped to eat **some** lunch.
8. live — Do you **live** on my street?
9. have — We **have** fun in gym every day.
10. said — Alex **said** he can walk home.

SORT THE SPELLING WORDS

Write the spelling words that have these sounds.

    1. **short a** sound
   2.–3. **short e** sound
   4.–6. **short i** sound
  7.–10. **short u** sound

REMEMBER THE SPELLING STRATEGY

Remember that some short vowel sounds are spelled with two vowels together: **ai** in **said** and **ee** in **been**.

Spelling ᵃⁿᵈ Phonics

Rhyming Words

Write the spelling word that completes each sentence. The word will rhyme with the underlined word.

1. Tell me who <u>won</u> when the game is ____.
2. I have plenty of <u>gum</u>, so I will give you ____.
3. Lie down on the <u>bed</u> and rest your ____.

Sounds and Letters

4. Write the word that spells the **short a** sound **a-consonant-e**.
5. Write the word that begins with a **/k/** sound.
6. Write the word that ends with a **/z/** sound but not the letter **z**.
7. Write the word that can have a **short i** sound or a **long i** sound.

USING THE Dictionary

A dictionary lists words in a-b-c order.

8.–10. Write these words in a-b-c order.

give   been   said

◆ ◆ ◆

Dictionary Check Be sure to check the a-b-c order of the words in your **Spelling Dictionary**.

Rhyming Words

1.

2.

3.

Sounds and Letters

4.

5.

6.

7.

Using the Dictionary

8.

9.

10.

give	come	does	done	been
head	some	live	have	said

Match the Shapes

1.

2.

Complete the Sequences

3.

4.

5.

6.

Use the Clues

7.

8.

9.

10.

Match the Shapes Write the spelling word that completes the sentence and matches the shape.

1. Julio and I will play ⬚⬚⬚⬚ songs for you.

2. What do you ⬚⬚⬚⬚ in your lunch bag today?

Complete the Sequences Write the spelling word that belongs in each group.

3. be, being, _____

4. say, saying, _____

5. do, did, _____

6. be born, _____, die

Use the Clues Write the spelling word that fits each clue.

7. This word can mean the opposite of "take away."

8. It is part of the body.

9. It means "do" and is used with **he, she,** and **it**.

10. This word can mean the opposite of "go."

Spelling and Writing

Proofread an Invitation

Four words are not spelled correctly in this invitation. Write the words correctly.

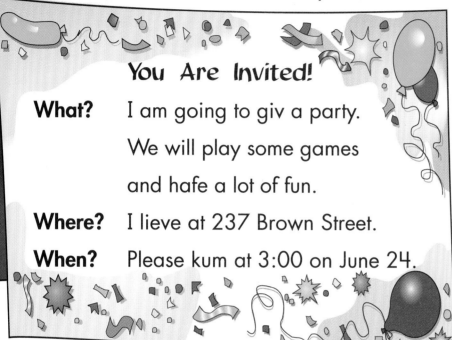

You Are Invited!

What?   I am going to giv a party.
We will play some games
and hafe a lot of fun.

Where?   I lieve at 237 Brown Street.

When?   Please kum at 3:00 on June 24.

Proofreading Marks

≡ Make a capital.

/ Make a small letter.

∧ Add something.

℘ Take out something.

⊙ Add a period.

⌗ New paragraph

(SP) Spelling error

Write an Invitation

Expository Writing

Write a party invitation. Make sure to tell

- what will happen.
- where it will happen.
- when it will happen.

Use as many spelling words as you can.

Writing Process

Prewriting
⇩
Drafting
⇩
Revising
⇩
Editing
⇩
Publishing

Proofread Your Writing During → Editing

Proofread your writing for spelling errors as part of the editing stage in the writing process. Be sure to check each word carefully. Use a dictionary to check spelling if you are not sure.

Vocabulary

Strategy Words

Review Words

1. _____

2. _____

3. _____

Preview Words

4. _____

5. _____

6. _____

Review Words: Short Vowel Sounds

Write a word from the box to complete each sentence.

and	fix	leg

1. I gave the books and the CD to Jen _____ Rico.

2. Bend each _____ before you run.

3. Please _____ the hole in the screen.

Preview Words: Short Vowel Sounds

Follow the directions to write a word from the box.

become	love	nothing

4. look – ok + ve = _____

5. noon – on + thing = _____

6. begin – gin + come = _____

Connections

Content Words

Math: Measurement

Write the word from the box that fits each clue.

guess	foot	inch	yard

1. This is equal to twelve inches. It is the length of a ruler.
2. This is equal to three feet. It is the length of a yardstick.
3. This means "to give an answer that you are not sure about."
4. One of these, plus eleven more, make a foot.

Apply the Spelling Strategy

Circle the content word you wrote in which two vowels spell the **short e** sound.

Math: Measurement

1.

2.

3.

4.

a-consonant-e

1. _____

2. _____

3. _____

4. _____

i-consonant-e

5. _____

6. _____

o-consonant-e

7. _____

8. _____

u-consonant-e

9. _____

10. _____

Spelling and Thinking

READ THE SPELLING WORDS

1. cute — That baby has a **cute** face.
2. wave — The children **wave** good-bye.
3. robe — My **robe** keeps me warm.
4. late — Don't be **late** for school.
5. mule — A **mule** is a big, slow animal.
6. tape — I **tape** the sign to the wall.
7. joke — The **joke** was very funny.
8. fire — Wood burns in a **fire**.
9. pipe — Water runs through that **pipe**.
10. base — Sean ran to first **base**.

SORT THE SPELLING WORDS

Write the spelling words that have these spelling patterns.

1.–4. **a-consonant-e**

5.–6. **i-consonant-e**

7.–8. **o-consonant-e**

9.–10. **u-consonant-e**

REMEMBER THE SPELLING STRATEGY

Remember that long vowel sounds can be spelled with the **vowel-consonant-e** pattern.

Spelling ᵃⁿᵈ Phonics

Rhyming Words

Write a spelling word that fits the sentence. The spelling word will rhyme with the underlined word.

1. We have a <u>date</u>. Don't be ____.
2. That girl plays the <u>flute</u>. She looks ____.
3. Don't put that old <u>tire</u> into the ____.
4. We made a paper <u>cape</u> with scissors and ____.

Beginning Sounds

Write the spelling word that begins with the same sound as the words in each group.

5. road, roll, rope, ____
6. music, mud, mug, ____
7. bake, bat, ball, ____

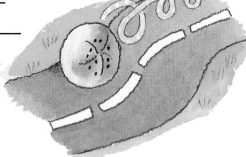

USING THE Dictionary

The words in a dictionary are in a-b-c order.

8.–10. Write these spelling words in a-b-c order.

joke   wave   pipe

◆ ◆ ◆

Dictionary Check Be sure to check the a-b-c order of the words in your **Spelling Dictionary**.

Rhyming Words

1. _____
2. _____
3. _____
4. _____

Beginning Sounds

5. _____
6. _____
7. _____

Using the Dictionary

8. _____
9. _____
10. _____

cute	wave	robe	late	mule
tape	joke	fire	pipe	base

Complete the Sentences

Write a spelling word to complete each sentence.

1. The _____ has packs on its back.
2. Did you see me steal third _____?
3. We listened to a _____ of the school band.

Complete the Story

Write the spelling words that complete the story.

Hurrah for the circus! We hurried to get ready. We did not want to get there __4.__. Once the show began, a clown told a very funny __5.__. Then she blew bubbles through a long __6.__ she pulled from a sack. I was thrilled when she began to __7.__ at us. Clowns do so many __8.__ and funny things in the circus!

My favorite person in the circus was the lion tamer. He walked to the center ring wearing a red __9.__. His act ended when he set a hoop on __10.__. Then all the lions jumped through the burning hoop.

Complete the Sentences

1. _____
2. _____
3. _____

Complete the Story

4. _____
5. _____
6. _____
7. _____
8. _____
9. _____
10. _____

Spelling and Writing

Proofread a Dialogue

Four words are not spelled correctly in this dialogue. Write the words correctly.

"Here is a cute joak," Jane said.

"What did the waive say to the water?"

"What?" asked Nate.

"Hi, tide," said Jane. "Here's one

more. If a frog got a flat tier or broke a

fuel piepe, whom would he call?"

"I know," said Nate. "A toad truck!"

Proofreading Marks

≡ Make a capital.

/ Make a small letter.

∧ Add something.

℔ Take out something.

⊙ Add a period.

⌗ New paragraph

ⓈⓅ Spelling error

Write a Dialogue

Narrative Writing

Think of two people. Write a chat they might have. Be sure to

- let your reader know who is speaking.
- use quotation marks (" ") to show the exact words of each speaker.

Use as many spelling words as you can.

Writing Process

Prewriting

⇩

Drafting

⇩

Revising

⇩

Proofread Your Writing During ▶ Editing

⇩

Publishing

Proofread your writing for spelling errors as part of the editing stage in the writing process. Be sure to check each word carefully. Use a dictionary to check spelling if you are not sure.

Vocabulary

Strategy Words

Review Words

1. _____

2. _____

3. _____

Preview Words

4. _____

5. _____

6. _____

Review Words: Vowel-Consonant-e

Write a word from the box for each clue.

bone	made	ride

1. It names something to do at a fair or carnival. It rhymes with **side**.

2. It can mean **did** or **earned**. It rhymes with **shade**.

3. It is part of the body. It rhymes with **tone**.

Preview Words: Vowel-Consonant-e

Write a word from the box to complete each analogy.

broke	face	size

4. **Fingers** are to **hand** as **eyes** are to

   _____.

5. **Tall** is to **height** as **large** is to _____.

6. **Ended** is to **began** as **fixed** is to

   _____.

TICKETS

Connections

Content Words

Science: Pond Life

Write the word from the box that fits each meaning.

| swamp | tadpole | toad | snail |

1. This word names an animal that has a shell and moves slowly. You might find it in your garden.
2. This word names a frog in the early stage of life.
3. This word names an animal that is like a frog. It has rough, dry skin.
4. This word names a wet place. Many animals live here.

Apply the Spelling Strategy

Circle the **vowel-consonant-e** pattern in one of the content words you wrote.

Science: Pond Life

1. _____
2. _____
3. _____
4. _____

Unit 7

1.

2.

Unit 8

3.

4.

Unit 9

5.

6.

7.

Unit 10

8.

Unit 11

9.

10.

Assessment and Review

Assessment Units 7–11

Each Assessment Word in the box fits one of the spelling strategies you have studied over the past five weeks. Read the spelling strategies. Then write each Assessment Word under the unit number it fits.

Unit 7
1.–2. The vowel sound you hear in **ball** and **talk** can be spelled **a**.

Unit 8
3.–4. A **consonant cluster** is two or more consonants together that make more than one sound: **gl** in **glad** and **dr** in **dress**.

Unit 9
5.–7. A **consonant cluster** is two or more consonants together that make more than one sound: **nk** in **bank**. A **consonant digraph** is two or more consonants together that make one new sound: **ng** in **ring**.

Unit 10
8. Some short vowel sounds are spelled with two vowels together.

Unit 11
9.–10. Long vowel sounds can be spelled with the **vowel-consonant-e** pattern.

cove
dead
sung
hate
salt
grip
tank
hall
flap
ink

Review Unit 7: Vowel Sound in ball

| all | talk | small | walk | call |

Write the spelling words that match the clues.

1. This word begins like **smell**. It rhymes with **tall**.
2. This word has four letters. It rhymes with **hall**.
3. This word begins with a vowel. It rhymes with **fall**.

Write the spelling word that fits each shape.

4.   5.

Review Unit 8: Consonant Clusters

| glad | grass | plant | front | class |

Answer each riddle with a spelling word.

6. I grow in the yard and get mowed.
7. I can grow in a pot on the windowsill.
8. I am the opposite of **back**.
9. I am the opposite of **sad**.
10. I am you and those in your schoolroom.

Unit 7

1.

2.

3.

4.

5.

Unit 8

6.

7.

8.

9.

10.

1.

2.

3.

4.

5.

6.

7.

8.

9.

10.

Review — Unit 9: nk, ng

bank	sing	drink	long	king

Write the spelling word that completes each sentence.

1. I save my coins. The money is in the _____.
2. Are you thirsty? Would you like a _____ of water?
3. I have an idea. Let's _____ a song together.
4. We will visit Grandpa. I haven't seen him for a _____ time.
5. That gold crown must belong to the _____.

Review — Unit 10: Short Vowel Sounds

said	some	been	does	have

Write the spelling word by adding the missing letters.

6. h __ v __

7. d __ __ s

8. __ ee __

Write the spelling word that fits each shape.

9. ☐☐☐☐

10. ☐☐☐▯

 Unit 11: Vowel-Consonant-e

late	joke	fire	cute	base

Write the correct spelling word for each sentence.

1. Did you laugh at Sherry's (base, joke)?
2. We'll roast hot dogs over the (late, fire).
3. That puppy is really (cute, fire).
4. Don't be (joke, late) for practice.
5. The (base, cute) of the lamp is made of brass.

 **Spelling Study Strategy**

Sorting by Sounds and Spellings

One way to practice spelling is to place words into groups according to a spelling pattern.

1. Work in groups of five. Choose some spelling words from Units 7–11.

2. Have each person write one of these labels at the top of a piece of paper:
   (1) Vowel Sound in **ball**
   (2) **gl, gr, pl, fl, fr, cl, dr, br**
   (3) **ng, nk**
   (4) Short Vowel Sound
   (5) Vowel-Consonant-**e**

3. Each person then writes a spelling word on the paper with the label that fits its spelling pattern.

4. Pass papers around and add other words to each list. Then go over each list together and check the spelling.

Unit 11

1. _____

2. _____

3. _____

4. _____

5. _____

Unit **12** enrichment

WRITER'S

A.

1. _____

2. _____

3. _____

4. _____

5. _____

6. _____

B. _____

7. _____

8. _____

9. _____

10. _____

Grammar, Usage, and Mechanics

Sentences That Tell, Sentences That Ask

A telling sentence makes a statement. It ends with a period.

> The grass is wet.

An asking sentence asks a question. It ends with a question mark.

> Is the grass wet?

Both kinds of sentences begin with a capital letter.

Practice **Activity**

A. What kind of sentence is each one below? Write **telling** or **asking**.

1. Does Mom know?   2. Who has a ball?
3. Those dogs are cute.   4. I will come, too.
5. Did Dan call?   6. The farm is flat.

B. Write the word that completes each sentence.

said	walk	plant	joke

7. Did you tell that funny _____?

8. Juan _____, "Yes, I will."

9. We can _____ home together.

10. Will the _____ grow soon?

78

WORKSHOP

Pair Up With a Partner!

Good writers always proofread their writing for spelling mistakes. Here's a strategy you can use to proofread your papers.

Work with a partner. Have the partner read your work out loud while you follow along. Ask the person to read slowly. You look at each word that your partner reads. Is the word spelled correctly?

Electronic Spelling

Computer Terms

Computers are fun to use. They allow you to write, draw, and play games.

Sometimes you want to write about computers. Your writing may include compound words that name things about computers. Compound words are words made from two shorter words. Spell these words carefully. Make sure that each small word is right. Then the compound word will be right.

Three compound words are misspelled. Spell them correctly. Write **OK** for the others.

1. starttup
2. dounload
3. desktop
4. keeboard
5. shortcut
6. network

Electronic Spelling

1. _____
2. _____
3. _____
4. _____
5. _____
6. _____

a-consonant-e

1. _____

2. _____

3. _____

ai

4. _____

5. _____

ay

6. _____

7. _____

8. _____

9. _____

10. _____

Spelling and Thinking

READ THE SPELLING WORDS

1.	safe	This is a **safe** place.
2.	day	What **day** of the week is it?
3.	rain	I can't run fast in the **rain**.
4.	say	Please **say** yes.
5.	play	Will you **play** catch with me?
6.	ate	Who **ate** the last plum?
7.	stay	Let's **stay** here for an hour.
8.	save	Everyone can help **save** water.
9.	may	You **may** come in.
10.	wait	I **wait** for the mail to come.

SORT THE SPELLING WORDS

1.–3. Write the spelling words with the **long a** sound spelled **a-consonant-e**.

4.–5. Write the spelling words with the **long a** sound spelled **ai**.

6.–10. Write the spelling words with the **long a** sound spelled **ay**.

REMEMBER THE SPELLING STRATEGY

Remember that the **long a** sound can be spelled in different ways: **a-consonant-e** in **save**, **ai** in **rain**, and **ay** in **day**.

Spelling and Phonics

Beginning and Ending Sounds ——·—·—

Write the spelling word that fits each clue.

1. It begins like **race** and ends like **tin**.
2. It begins like **stop** and ends like **pay**.
3. It begins like **wave** and ends like **sit**.
4. It begins like **dark** and ends like **say**.
5. It begins like **plan** and ends like **way**.

Word Structure ———————

6. Change the last letter in **map** to make this spelling word.
7. Change the first two letters in **live** to make this spelling word.
8. Drop one letter in **late** to make this spelling word.

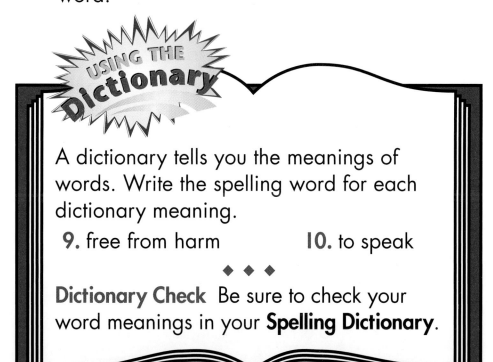

USING THE Dictionary

A dictionary tells you the meanings of words. Write the spelling word for each dictionary meaning.

9. free from harm   10. to speak

◆ ◆ ◆

Dictionary Check Be sure to check your word meanings in your **Spelling Dictionary**.

Beginning and Ending Sounds

1. _____

2. _____

3. _____

4. _____

5. _____

Word Structure

6. _____

7. _____

8. _____

Using the Dictionary

9. _____

10. _____

safe	day	rain	say	play
ate	stay	save	may	wait

Complete the Sentences

Complete the Sentences Write the spelling word that completes each sentence.

1. Willa spent her money. I am going to _____ mine.

2. I will eat my apple now. Brett already _____ his.

3. I did not hear her. What did Kate _____ about that book?

Complete the Story Write the spelling words that complete the story.

One __4.__, D.J. wanted to go outside. She looked out the window. It was raining very hard. There was thunder, too. D.J. had to __5.__ inside. She did not want to __6.__ for the __7.__ to stop. She asked, "Please, Dad, __8.__ I go outside to __9.__?"

"No," said her dad. "It is not a good time to be outside. Stay inside. Here you are __10.__ from the storm."

D.J. said, "I know an indoor game we can play!"

Complete the Sentences

1. _____

2. _____

3. _____

Complete the Story

4. _____

5. _____

6. _____

7. _____

8. _____

9. _____

10. _____

Spelling and Writing

Proofread a Letter

Four words are not spelled correctly in this letter. Write the words correctly.

Dear Dale,

Our class collects cans one dey every week. We use the money we make to save the rane forest. Don't wate to join us. Then you can saiy that you helped save land!

Your friend,

Jamal

Write a Letter

Persuasive Writing

Write to a friend. Ask him or her to join you in doing some good work. Be sure to tell

- what you are doing.
- what you are working for.
- why your friend should help.

Use as many spelling words as you can.

Writing Process

Prewriting

⇩

Drafting

⇩

Revising

⇩

Proofread Your Writing During Editing

⇩

Publishing

Proofread your writing for spelling errors as part of the editing stage in the writing process. Be sure to check each word carefully. Use a dictionary to check spelling if you are not sure.

Vocabulary

Strategy Words

Review Words

1. _____

2. _____

3. _____

Preview Words

4. _____

5. _____

6. _____

Review Words:
Long a Spelled a-Consonant-e, ai, ay

Write a word from the box for each clue.

ape	bake	game

1. This word names many kinds of play.
2. This action is part of making bread or cake.
3. This word rhymes with **tape**.

Preview Words:
Long a Spelled a-Consonant-e, ai, ay

Write a word from the box for each meaning.

always	plain	space

4. This word means "room" or "an empty place."
5. This word means "not fancy."
6. This word means "every time" or "forever."

Connections

Content Words

Health: Foods

Write words from the box that complete the paragraph.

grape	snacks	raisin	apple

　　Try to eat ___1.___ that are good for you. Fruit makes a great snack. One fruit that grows on a vine is the ___2.___. When it is dried, it becomes a ___3.___. One fruit that grows on a tree is an ___4.___. Grapes, raisins, and apples have many vitamins. They give you energy, too.

Apply the Spelling Strategy

Circle the two content words you wrote that contain the **long a** sound.

Health: Foods

1. _____

2. _____

3. _____

4. _____

ee

1. _____

2. _____

3. _____

4. _____

5. _____

ea

6. _____

7. _____

8. _____

9. _____

10. _____

Spelling and Thinking

READ THE SPELLING WORDS

1.	sea	Fish swim in the **sea**.
2.	week	The school **week** begins today.
3.	eat	You may **eat** this apple.
4.	beef	Dad likes **beef** for dinner.
5.	neat	Please keep your room **neat**.
6.	need	I **need** to drink some water.
7.	seat	Have a **seat** on the sofa.
8.	seem	Those people **seem** nice.
9.	read	I can **read** this book.
10.	seen	Have you **seen** my cat?

SORT THE SPELLING WORDS

The words on the spelling list have the **long e** sound.

1.–5. Write the spelling words with the **long e** sound spelled **ee**.

6.–10. Write the spelling words with the **long e** sound spelled **ea**.

REMEMBER THE SPELLING STRATEGY

Remember that the **long e** sound can be spelled in different ways: **ee** in **seen** and **ea** in **eat**.

Spelling and Phonics

Sound and Letter Patterns

Follow the directions to write a spelling word.

1. seen – n + m = ____
2. sea – a + en = ____
3. really – lly + d = ____
4. weed – d + k = ____
5. sell – ll + a = ____

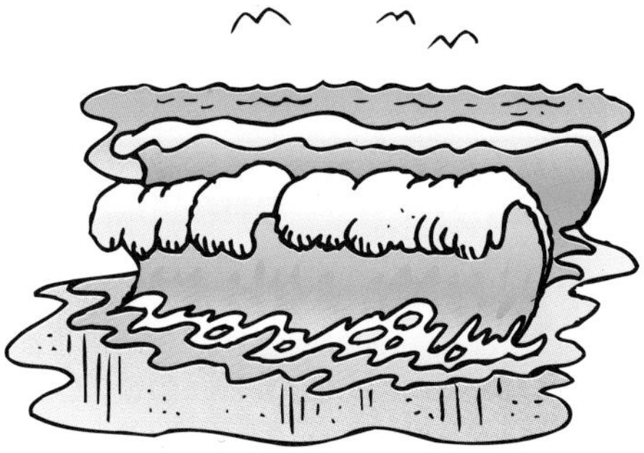

Beginning and Ending Sounds

6. Write the spelling word that begins like **need** and ends like **meat**.
7. Write the spelling word that begins with the **long e** sound.
8. Write the spelling word that begins like **see** and ends like **beat**.

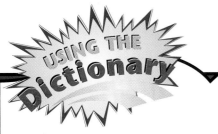

Using the Dictionary

A dictionary tells you the meanings of words. Write the spelling word for each dictionary meaning.

9. kind of meat
10. must have

◆ ◆ ◆

Dictionary Check Be sure to check your word meanings in your **Spelling Dictionary**.

Sound and Letter Patterns

1. ____
2. ____
3. ____
4. ____
5. ____

Beginning and Ending Sounds

6. ____
7. ____
8. ____

Using the Dictionary

9. ____
10. ____

Spelling and Reading

sea	week	eat	beef	neat
need	seat	seem	read	seen

Solve the Analogies

Write a spelling word to complete each analogy.

1. **Pig** is to **pork** as **cow** is to _____.
2. **Cup** is to **drink** as **fork** is to _____.
3. **Fat** is to **thin** as **messy** is to _____.
4. **Video** is to **watch** as **book** is to _____.
5. **Soil** is to **water** as **land** is to _____.

Complete the Paragraph

Write the spelling words that complete the paragraph.

Dad and I take a bus ride when we want to see Grandma. We can go any day of the __6.__. I like to ride in the back __7.__. From the window, I have __8.__ trucks, bridges, and tall buildings. When we __9.__ to go home, we take the bus again. Does it __10.__ like riding on a bus is fun? It is!

Solve the Analogies

1. _____
2. _____
3. _____
4. _____
5. _____

Complete the Paragraph

6. _____
7. _____
8. _____
9. _____
10. _____

88

Spelling and Writing

Proofread a Book Report

Four words are not spelled correctly in this book report. Write the words correctly.

A Sea Story

You should reed this book! It is called <u>Sea Life</u>. It is by Ian Whitelaw. It tells about sea animals you have never sean. Some are so strange! They don't even seam real. You will learn what they look like and what they eet.

Proofreading Marks

≡ Make a capital.

/ Make a small letter.

∧ Add something.

℮ Take out something.

⊙ Add a period.

⌗ New paragraph

ⓢⓟ Spelling error

Write a Book Report

Persuasive Writing

Write a book report. Explain why someone else should read the book. Be sure to tell

- the title and author.
- what the book is about.
- why it is worth reading.

Use as many spelling words as you can.

Writing Process

Prewriting

⇩

Drafting

⇩

Revising

⇩

Proofread Your Writing During ▶ **Editing**

⇩

Publishing

Proofread your writing for spelling errors as part of the editing stage in the writing process. Be sure to check each word carefully. Use a dictionary to check spelling if you are not sure.

Vocabulary

Strategy Words

Review Words

1. _____

2. _____

3. _____

Preview Words

4. _____

5. _____

6. _____

Review Words: Long e Spelled ee, ea

Write a word from the box for each clue.

beet	deep	easy

1. This word means the opposite of "hard."
2. This word names something you can eat.
3. This word can describe a hole.

Preview Words: Long e Spelled ee, ea

Write a word from the box by adding the missing letters.

beaver	stream	street

4. str __ a __
5. be __ v __ r
6. s __ r __ et

Connections

Content Words

Language Arts: Exact Words

Write the word from the box that has the same meaning as the underlined word or words.

leap	prance	bounce	romp

1. The squirrel seems to <u>jump</u> from one tree to another.
2. I can <u>throw down and catch</u> a ball for a long time.
3. The little children laugh and <u>play</u> in the yard.
4. Come look over the fence! Watch the horse <u>lift its feet high</u>.

Apply the Spelling Strategy

Circle the letters that spell the **long e** sound in one of the content words you wrote.

Language Arts: Exact Words

1. _____
2. _____
3. _____
4. _____

Unit **15**
Long i: y,
i-Consonant-e

Spelling and Thinking

two-letter words with y

1.

2.

three-letter words with y

3.

4.

5.

6.

7.

i-consonant-e

8.

9.

10.

READ THE SPELLING WORDS

1.	my	I put **my** seat next to yours.
2.	try	I will **try** to call later.
3.	mile	Mom runs one **mile** each day.
4.	cry	I **cry** when I feel bad.
5.	fry	Jan will **fry** the meat.
6.	nice	That **nice** man helped me.
7.	by	This story is **by** Ron.
8.	sky	The **sky** is gray today.
9.	fine	What a **fine** day for a picnic!
10.	dry	The shirt can **dry** in the sun.

SORT THE SPELLING WORDS

1.–2. Write the two-letter spelling words that spell the **long i** sound with **y**.

3.–7. Write the three-letter spelling words that spell the **long i** sound with **y**.

8.–10. Write the spelling words that spell the **long i** sound with **i-consonant-e**.

REMEMBER THE SPELLING STRATEGY

Remember that the **long i** sound can be spelled in different ways: **y** in **sky** and **i-consonant-e** in **fine**.

Spelling and Phonics

Rhyming Words

Write a spelling word that fits each sentence. The spelling word will rhyme with the underlined word.

1. On a hot day, a little <u>ice</u> feels very ____.
2. I don't know <u>why</u>, but I left ____ bat at home.
3. This dog is <u>mine</u>! He is ____!

Word Structure

Change the underlined letter to make a spelling word. Write the spelling word.

4. d<u>a</u>y   5. s<u>a</u>y

Word Meanings

Write the spelling word that fits each clue.

6. It is 5,280 feet.
7. Tears fall when you do this.

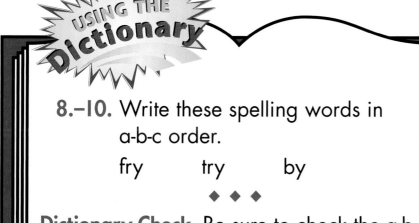

USING THE Dictionary

8.–10. Write these spelling words in a-b-c order.

fry   try   by

◆ ◆ ◆

Dictionary Check Be sure to check the a-b-c order of the words in your **Spelling Dictionary**.

Rhyming Words

1.

2.

3.

Word Structure

4.

5.

Word Meanings

6.

7.

Using the Dictionary

8.

9.

10.

Spelling and Reading

my	try	mile	cry	fry
nice	by	sky	fine	dry

Complete the Sentences

1.
2.
3.
4.
5.

Replace the Words

6.
7.
8.
9.
10.

Complete the Sentences Write the spelling word that completes each sentence.

1. Crack the egg and throw away the shell. Then put the egg in a pan to _____.
2. Let go of the balloon. Watch it drift off into the _____.
3. It is more than five blocks to school. It is at least a _____ away.
4. I know you are sad we lost the game. Try not to _____.
5. That book does not belong to you. It is _____ book.

Replace the Words Write the spelling word that could best take the place of the underlined word or words.

6. The book is <u>next to</u> the vase.
7. I will <u>do my best</u> to win the race.
8. That <u>kind</u> person helped me when I fell.
9. I always feel <u>great</u> when I play ball.
10. These clothes are <u>not wet</u>.

94

Spelling and Writing

Proofread a Paragraph

Four words are not spelled correctly in this paragraph. Write the words correctly.

Camping Is Fun

You can have a fyne time camping if you do these things. First, go when it is dry. Find a place where you can look up at the ski. Keep warm bi making a fire. If you bring the right food and gear, you can even triy cooking over the fire.

Write a Paragraph

Expository Writing

Write about something you like to do. Give advice on how to do it right. Include

- where to do it.
- when to do it.
- how to do it.

Use as many spelling words as you can.

Writing Process

Prewriting

⇩

Drafting

⇩

Revising

⇩

Proofread Your Writing During ▶ **Editing**

⇩

Publishing

Proofread your writing for spelling errors as part of the editing stage in the writing process. Be sure to check each word carefully. Use a dictionary to check spelling if you are not sure.

Vocabulary

Strategy Words

Review Words

1. _____
2. _____
3. _____

Preview Words

4. _____
5. _____
6. _____

Review Words: Long i Spelled y, i-Consonant-e

Write a word from the box to complete each analogy.

bike	hide	line

1. **Four wheels** is to **car** as **two wheels** is to _____.
2. **Round** is to **circle** as **straight** is to _____.
3. **Win** is to **lose** as **show** is to _____.

Preview Words: Long i Spelled y, i-Consonant-e

Change the underlined letters to make each word from the box. Write the word.

alike	housefly	prize

4. house<u>boat</u>
5. <u>p</u>lace
6. <u>s</u>li<u>d</u>e

Connections

Content Words

Math: Money

Write the word from the box that fits each definition.

coin	nickel	dime	penny

1. It is the smallest coin. Two nickels equal this.
2. Five pennies equal this.
3. It is worth the least amount. One cent is the same as this.
4. This can be a dime. It can also be a penny or a nickel.

Apply the Spelling Strategy

Circle the content word you wrote that has the **long i** sound.

Math: Money

1. _____
2. _____
3. _____
4. _____

long o spelled o

1. _____

2. _____

3. _____

4. _____

long o spelled oa

5. _____

6. _____

long o spelled ow

7. _____

8. _____

9. _____

10. _____

Spelling and Thinking

READ THE SPELLING WORDS

1.	old	She is eight years **old**.
2.	know	Do you **know** the answer?
3.	road	Sarah lives on this **road**.
4.	cold	It can be **cold** in March.
5.	grow	We will **grow** beans here.
6.	hold	I can **hold** this big book.
7.	low	The nest is on a **low** branch.
8.	told	I **told** the story to Ken.
9.	own	I **own** a bike and a helmet.
10.	coat	My **coat** keeps me warm.

SORT THE SPELLING WORDS

1.–4. Write the spelling words with the **long o** sound spelled **o**.

5.–6. Write the spelling words with the **long o** sound spelled **oa**.

7.–10. Write the spelling words with the **long o** sound spelled **ow**.

REMEMBER THE SPELLING STRATEGY

Remember that the **long o** sound can be spelled in different ways: **o** in **old, oa** in **coat,** and **ow** in **low**.

Spelling and Phonics

Sound and Letter Patterns

Follow the directions to write a spelling word.

1. tip – ip + old = ＿＿＿
2. row – w + ad = ＿＿＿

Word Structure

3. Change the first letter in **snow** to make a spelling word.
4. Change two letters in **grip** to make a spelling word.
5. Change two letters in **help** to make a spelling word.

Word Groups

Write the spelling word that belongs in each group.

6. hot, warm, ＿＿＿
7. high, medium, ＿＿＿

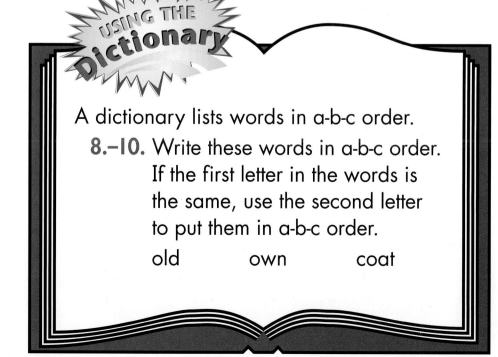

USING THE Dictionary

A dictionary lists words in a-b-c order.

8.–10. Write these words in a-b-c order. If the first letter in the words is the same, use the second letter to put them in a-b-c order.

old   own   coat

old	know	road	cold	grow
hold	low	told	own	coat

Solve the Analogies

1.
2.
3.
4.

Complete the Sentences

5.

6.

7.

8.

9.

10.

Solve the Analogies Write the spelling word that completes each analogy.

1. **Five** is to **young** as **seventy-five** is to _____.
2. **Neat** is to **messy** as **high** is to _____.
3. **Warm** is to **hot** as **chilly** is to _____.
4. **Fall** is to **rise** as **drop** is to _____.

Complete the Sentences Write the spelling word that completes each sentence.

5. I do not have a bike, but I have my _____ sled.
6. I could not hear you, but Brian _____ me what you said.
7. When it is cold outside, I wear mittens, a scarf, a hat, and a _____.
8. A rose can't _____ in this cold weather.
9. Please turn left here. This _____ leads to my house.
10. I _____ a boy on your team.

Spelling  Writing

Proofread a Story

Four words are not spelled correctly in this story.
Write the words correctly.

A Seal Story

Sam Seal got out of the water. He was cold.
Pete Penguin said, "You need a cote! I knoaw
where to get you one!"

"No, I don't," Sam toald Pete. "I've
already got my oan! It's wet and smooth.
Most of the time it keeps me very warm."

Write a Story

Narrative Writing

Write a story. Be sure your story has
- characters (people or animals).
- events (things that happen).
- a setting or place where the events happen.

Use as many spelling words as you can.

Proofread Your Writing During → **Editing**

Proofread your writing for spelling errors as part
of the editing stage in the writing process. Be sure
to check each word carefully. Use a dictionary to
check spelling if you are not sure.

Writing Process

Prewriting

Drafting

Revising

Editing

Publishing

Vocabulary

Strategy Words

Review Words

1. _____

2. _____

3. _____

Preview Words

4. _____

5. _____

6. _____

Review Words:
Long o Spelled o, oa, ow

Write a word from the box for each clue.

ago	go	no

1. It has two syllables.
2. It is the opposite of **yes**.
3. It is the opposite of **stop**.

Preview Words:
Long o Spelled o, oa, ow

Write a word from the box to complete each sentence.

below	foam	odor

4. The tips of the waves have some _____ on them.
5. There was a strange _____ coming from the stove.
6. The pile of books is _____ the desk.

Connections

Content Words

Health: Diseases

Write the word from the box that matches each clue.

ill	mumps	throat	rash

1. This word has a double consonant. It means the same as **sick**.

2. This word rhymes with **dash**. You get this when you have chicken pox.

3. This word ends with **s**. Your cheeks will get bigger if you get this.

4. This word contains the small word **oat**. Sometimes this hurts when you have a cold.

Apply the Spelling Strategy

Circle the letters that spell the **long o** sound in one of the content words you wrote.

Health: Diseases

1. _____

2. _____

3. _____

4. _____

Spelling and Thinking

k and ck

1. _____

c or k

2. _____

3. _____

4. _____

5. _____

6. _____

ck

7. _____

8. _____

9. _____

10. _____

READ THE SPELLING WORDS

1.	cook	The **cook** stirs the soup.
2.	sick	Pete is **sick** with the flu.
3.	cave	Many bats live in that **cave**.
4.	kiss	I **kiss** the baby on her cheek.
5.	rock	Never throw a **rock**.
6.	cake	Please give me a piece of **cake**.
7.	kick	I can **kick** the ball hard.
8.	lock	Does the key fit this **lock**?
9.	look	We **look** at the stars above.
10.	luck	Good **luck** in the race!

SORT THE SPELLING WORDS

1. Write the spelling word with the /**k**/ sound spelled with both **k** and **ck**.

2.–6. Write the other spelling words with a /**k**/ sound spelled **c** or **k**.

7.–10. Write the other spelling words with the /**k**/ sound spelled **ck**.

REMEMBER THE SPELLING STRATEGY

Remember that the /**k**/ sound can be spelled in different ways: **c** in **cave**, **k** in **look**, and **ck** in **sick**.

Spelling and Phonics

Word Structure

1. Write the spelling word that begins with the /**k**/ sound and contains a double consonant.

2. Write the spelling word that begins and ends with the /**k**/ sound and contains a double vowel.

3. Write the spelling word that contains the **long a** sound and has the /**k**/ sound just once.

Rhyming Words

Write the spelling word that fits the sentence. The spelling word will rhyme with the underlined word.

4. <u>Pick</u> a good doctor when you are ____.

5. Let's ____ at the pictures in my <u>book</u>.

6. We can <u>bake</u> a ____ for the birthday party.

7. The small ____ in my <u>sock</u> hurt my foot.

USING THE Dictionary

A dictionary lists words in a-b-c order.

8.–10. Write these words in a-b-c order.

    luck   lock   kick

◆ ◆ ◆

Dictionary Check Be sure to check the a-b-c order of the words in your **Spelling Dictionary**.

Word Structure

1. _____

2. _____

3. _____

Rhyming Words

4. _____

5. _____

6. _____

7. _____

Using the Dictionary

8. _____

9. _____

10. _____

Spelling and Reading

cook	sick	cave	kiss	rock
cake	kick	lock	look	luck

Complete the Sentences

Write the spelling word that will complete each sentence.

1. Did you remember to _____ the door when you left the house?
2. I can _____ noodles and corn for our dinner tonight.
3. How many candles are on your birthday _____?

Complete the Paragraph

Write spelling words to complete the paragraph.

On January 24, 1848, James Marshall saw some shiny flakes in the river. He hit them with a __4.__. The flakes became flat! Marshall had found gold. Soon people came from far and near to __5.__ for gold. They slept in tents. Some tried to find a warm, dry, dark __6.__. No wonder many miners got __7.__. Most people had no __8.__ finding gold. But some miners struck it rich. They would __9.__ up their heels when they found gold. They would even __10.__ the gold!

Complete the Sentences

1. _____
2. _____
3. _____

Complete the Paragraph

4. _____
5. _____
6. _____
7. _____
8. _____
9. _____
10. _____

Spelling and Writing

Proofread a Book Report

Four words are not spelled correctly in this book report. Write the words correctly.

An Exciting Book

The Haunted Cave, by Christopher Pike, is about some kids who loock inside a cave. They have bad luk. There is more than just rok in the cave. They are almost sik with fear! This is an exciting book.

Proofreading Marks

≡ Make a capital.

/ Make a small letter.

∧ Add something.

ℒ Take out something.

⊙ Add a period.

⌗ New paragraph

🆂🅿 Spelling error

Write a Book Report

Expository Writing

Tell about a book you liked. Be sure your book report tells

- the name of the book.
- the author of the book.
- a little about what happens.

Use as many spelling words as you can.

Proofread Your Writing During

Writing Process

Prewriting
⇩
Drafting
⇩
Revising
⇩
Editing
⇩
Publishing

Proofread your writing for spelling errors as part of the editing stage in the writing process. Be sure to check each word carefully. Use a dictionary to check spelling if you are not sure.

Unit 17 enrichment

Vocabulary

Strategy Words

Review Words

1. _____

2. _____

3. _____

Preview Words

4. _____

5. _____

6. _____

Review Words: /k/ Spelled c, k, ck

Write a word from the box to complete each analogy.

back	cat	keep

1. **Sick** is to **ill** as **save** is to _____.
2. **Toy** is to **doll** as **pet** is to _____.
3. **Up** is to **down** as **front** is to _____.

Preview Words: /k/ Spelled c, k, ck

Follow the directions to write a word from the box.

bucket	carry	peak

4. cart – t + ry = _____
5. bush – sh + cket = _____
6. peel – el + ak = _____

Connections

Content Words

Language Arts: Puzzles

Write the word from the box that matches each clue.

cartoon	puzzle	riddle	maze

1. This puts words and pictures together. It will make you smile or laugh.
2. You need to find your way through this. It twists and turns.
3. This is something you put together. One kind is a crossword. Another is a jigsaw.
4. This is like a game with words. You guess the answer.

Apply the Spelling Strategy

Circle the letter that spells the /**k**/ sound in one of the content words you wrote.

Language Arts: Puzzles

1.

2.

3.

4.

Unit 13

1. _____

2. _____

Unit 14

3. _____

4. _____

Unit 15

5. _____

6. _____

Unit 16

7. _____

8. _____

Unit 17

9. _____

10. _____

Assessment and Review

Assessment   Units 13–17

Each Assessment Word in the box fits one of the spelling strategies you have studied over the past five weeks. Read the spelling strategies. Then write each Assessment Word under the unit number it fits.

Unit 13 _____

1.–2. The **long a** sound can be spelled in different ways: **a-consonant-e** in **save, ai** in **rain,** and **ay** in **day**.

Unit 14 _____

3.–4. The **long e** sound can be spelled in different ways: **ee** in **seen** and **ea** in **eat**.

Unit 15 _____

5.–6. The **long i** sound can be spelled in different ways: **y** in **sky** and **i-consonant-e** in **fine**.

Unit 16 _____

7.–8. The **long o** sound can be spelled in different ways: **o** in **old, oa** in **coat,** and **ow** in **low**.

Unit 17 _____

9.–10. The **/k/** sound can be spelled in different ways: **c** in **cave, k** in **look,** and **ck** in **sick**.

| boat |
| sheet |
| sack |
| spy |
| tea |
| ray |
| mask |
| lime |
| gold |
| jail |

Unit 13: Long a Spelled a–Consonant-e, ai, ay

may	rain	say	play	wait

Write the spelling word by adding letters.

1. m __ y   **2.** s __ __

3. __ ait

Write the spelling word
that fits each shape.

4.

5.

Unit 14: Long e Spelled ee, ea

eat	read	seem	week	need

Write the spelling words to complete the paragraph.

The first __6.__ of each month our class chooses
new books to __7.__ . I hurry home with my book.
After I __8.__ my dinner, I __9.__ to find a
good, quiet spot. I __10.__ to read
better when it is quiet. I like to
read books about dinosaurs
and children who live in
other countries.

Unit 13

1. _____

2. _____

3. _____

4. _____

5. _____

Unit 14

6. _____

7. _____

8. _____

9. _____

10. _____

1. _____

2. _____

3. _____

4. _____

5. _____

6. _____

7. _____

8. _____

9. _____

10. _____

Review Unit 15: Long i Spelled y,
i-Consonant-e

my	try	nice	fine	by

1.–2. Write the two spelling words in which the **long i** sound comes in the middle of the word.

Write the spelling word that fits each shape.

3. 　　　　4. 　　　　5.

Review Unit 16: Long o Spelled o, oa, ow

told	coat	own	know	old

Replace each underlined word or words with a spelling word that means the same thing.

6. My mother <u>ordered</u> me to come in out of the rain.

7. I <u>remember</u> all my math facts.

8. In ten years, my brand new bike will be <u>worn out</u>.

9. When the day is cold, I wear my <u>jacket</u> to keep warm.

10. Did you know that I <u>have</u> a pet hamster named Fluffy?

 **Review** **Unit 17: /k/ Spelled c, k, ck**

cook	kiss	lock	cake	look

Some words are often used in pairs. Write the spelling word that completes each pair.

1. hug and _____

2. ice cream and _____

3. _____ and key

4. _____ and listen

5. _____ and clean

 **Spelling Study Strategy**

Go Fish

Practicing your spelling words can be fun if you make it into a game. Here is an idea you can try.

1. Make two sets of word cards so that you have two cards for every word.

2. Mix up the cards and give five cards to each person. Put the rest of the cards in a pile. If you have cards that match, put them down on the table.

3. Ask someone for a word that matches one in your hand. Spell the word out loud and say the word. If your friend has the word, you take it. If the person you ask does not have the word, choose a card from the pile.

4. Take turns.

5. Put your word pairs on the table. The first one to put all his or her cards on the table wins the game.

Unit 17

1. _____

2. _____

3. _____

4. _____

5. _____

WRITER'S

Grammar, Usage, and Mechanics

Commands and Exclamations

One kind of sentence gives a command. It usually ends with a period.

Get a dictionary.

Another kind of sentence shows strong feelings. It ends with an exclamation point.

What an odd word!

Practice Activity

A. Which sentences below are commands? Write **command** if the sentence is a command. Write **no** if it is not a command.

1. Is that your watch?
2. Hold out your hand.
3. Write me a nice letter.
4. I like to eat beef.

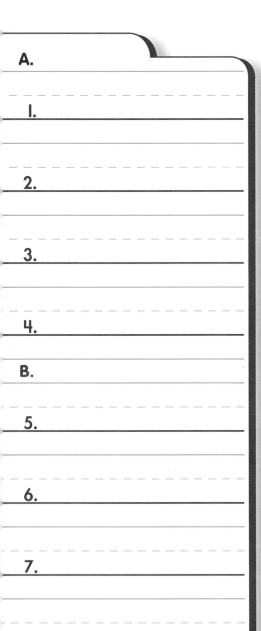

B. Some of these sentences show strong feeling, and some do not. Write the mark you would use to end each sentence.

5. Help me
6. Stay with me for a while
7. Go to the store
8. Don't touch that

A.

___
1. ___
___
2. ___
___
3. ___
___
4. ___
B.
___
5. ___
___
6. ___
___
7. ___
___
8. ___

WORKSHOP

One at a Time!

Good writers always proofread their writing for spelling mistakes. Here's a strategy that you should try. Look for one kind of mistake. For example, you might begin by looking for common spelling mistakes. When you have finished, look for mistakes in capital letters. Next, look for mistakes in words that are alike, such as **there** and **their**.

Electronic Spelling

Spell Checkers

Many computers have spell checkers. They can help you, but they do not find all kinds of mistakes. A writer may spell a word correctly, but it's the wrong word.

A computer checked the spelling of these sentences. Find the mistakes in spelling that the computer missed. Write the words correctly.

1. I will go two camp.
2. My bike is knew.
3. I ate an our ago.
4. Sea you soon!
5. Look buy the door.
6. I no the answer.

Electronic Spelling

1. _____
2. _____
3. _____
4. _____
5. _____
6. _____

Spelling and Thinking

consonant clusters with l

1. _____
2. _____
3. _____
4. _____
5. _____

consonant clusters with r

6. _____
7. _____
8. _____
9. _____
10. _____

READ THE SPELLING WORDS

1. fly   Birds **fly** south in winter.
2. clean   Let's **clean** that dirty sink.
3. sleep   I **sleep** on that cot.
4. free   I got a **free** ride on the pony.
5. grade   Are you in second **grade**?
6. drive   Bill can **drive** a motorboat.
7. train   We ride the **train** to Portland.
8. tree   This **tree** has very deep roots.
9. please   Will you **please** sit down?
10. slow   My watch is **slow**.

SORT THE SPELLING WORDS

The words on the spelling list have consonant clusters.

1.–5. Write the spelling words that are spelled with consonant clusters with **l**.

6.–10. Write the spelling words that are spelled with consonant clusters with **r**.

REMEMBER THE SPELLING STRATEGY

Remember that **consonant clusters** with **l** and **r** are heard at the beginning of the words **fly** and **free**.

Spelling and Phonics

Word Structure

Replace the underlined letters to write a spelling word.

1. <u>kn</u>ow
2. fr<u>om</u>
3. s<u>t</u>eep
4. g<u>l</u>ide
5. clea<u>r</u>

Rhyming Words

Write the spelling word that best completes each sentence. The word you write will rhyme with the underlined word.

6. The farmer's <u>grain</u> was shipped on a _____.

7. I scraped my <u>knee</u> on the bark of that big _____.

8. If Mom will _____, we can <u>arrive</u> there on time.

Using the Dictionary

The two words at the top of every dictionary page are called **guide words**. The guide words are the first and last words defined on that page. Write the spelling word that would be on the same page as these pairs of guide words.

9. or • prance
10. fine • footstep

Spelling and Reading

fly	clean	sleep	free	grade
drive	train	tree	please	slow

Complete the Paragraph

1. _____

2. _____

3. _____

4. _____

5. _____

6. _____

Solve the Analogies

7. _____

8. _____

9. _____

10. _____

Complete the Paragraph Write the spelling words that complete the paragraph.

Long ago, it was harder to travel than it is today. People rode in open wagons or on horses. Trips were long, __1.__, and dirty. Today things are very different. People can __2.__ cars down wide highways. They can __3.__ in planes from coast to coast, or speed along by __4.__. Besides being fast, these kinds of travel are also __5.__. Still, they all cost money. None of them are __6.__.

Solve the Analogies Write a spelling word to complete each analogy.

7. **Morning** is to **wake** as **night** is to _____.

8. **Fading** is to **fade** as **grading** is to _____.

9. **Pea** is to **vegetable** as **oak** is to _____.

10. **Good-bye** is to **hello** as **thank you** is to _____.

Spelling and Writing

Proofread a Paragraph

Four words are not spelled correctly in this paragraph. Write the words correctly.

Sky Ride

    I took my first plane ride ever. I had been on a trane and in a car, but I was afraid to flie. Once we got in the sky, I felt fine. I even felt feree. We were high above every tree and house. Soon I felt so calm that I went to sleap!

Proofreading Marks

≡	Make a capital.
/	Make a small letter.
∧	Add something.
ℒ	Take out something.
⊙	Add a period.
#	New paragraph
SP	Spelling error

Write a Paragraph

Narrative Writing

Tell about something you did for the first time. Be sure to

- say what was new.
- tell what you did, saw, or felt.

Use as many spelling words as you can.

Proofread Your Writing During Editing

Proofread your writing for spelling errors as part of the editing stage in the writing process. Be sure to check each word carefully. Use a dictionary to check spelling if you are not sure.

Writing Process

Prewriting

⇩

Drafting

⇩

Revising

⇩

Editing

⇩

Publishing

119

Vocabulary

Strategy Words

Review Words

1. _____

2. _____

3. _____

Preview Words

4. _____

5. _____

6. _____

Review Words: Consonant Clusters

Write a word from the box to replace the underlined word or words.

crash	plum	slip

1. We pick a <u>fruit</u> from the tree.

2. A <u>loud sound</u> came from the kitchen.

3. Be sure not to <u>slide and fall</u> on that ice.

Preview Words: Consonant Clusters

Write the word from the box that fits each clue.

cloudy	drugstore	slowly

4. This word is made up of two smaller words.

5. This word contains one smaller word and the ending **-ly**.

6. This word begins like **clam** and ends like **body**.

Connections

Content Words

Health: Teeth

Health: Teeth

Write the word from the box that matches each definition.

dental	floss	jaw	gum

1. a thin thread used to clean between the teeth
2. a part of the body that helps open and close the mouth
3. a part of the mouth that supports each tooth
4. having to do with teeth

Health: Teeth

1. _____

2. _____

3. _____

4. _____

Apply the Spelling Strategy

Circle the letters that make up the consonant cluster in one of the content words you wrote.

three letters

1. _____

2. _____

3. _____

4. _____

four letters

5. _____

6. _____

7. _____

five letters

8. _____

9. _____

10. _____

Spelling and Thinking

READ THE SPELLING WORDS

1.	one	I have just **one** brother.
2.	two	One dime equals **two** nickels.
3.	three	I am one of **three** children.
4.	four	One quart is **four** cups.
5.	five	Annie is **five** years old.
6.	six	I can check out **six** books.
7.	seven	One week has **seven** days.
8.	eight	I go to bed at **eight** o'clock.
9.	nine	Four plus five is **nine**.
10.	ten	Nick counts from one to **ten**.

SORT THE SPELLING WORDS

1.–4. Write the number words that are spelled with three letters.

5.–7. Write the number words that are spelled with four letters.

8.–10. Write the number words that are spelled with five letters.

REMEMBER THE SPELLING STRATEGY

Remember that there is a word name for each number. It is important to spell number words correctly.

Word Analysis

Write the spelling word that fits each clue.

1. It has two syllables.
2. It has the **long e** sound spelled **ee**.
3. It sounds the same as the word **for**.
4. It has the **short i** sound.
5. It has the **long a** sound but no letter **a**.

Sound and Letter Patterns

Write the spelling word that fits each clue.

6. It starts like **tea** and ends like **who**.
7. It starts like **nice** and ends like **twine**.
8. It starts like **test** and ends like **hen**.

USING THE Dictionary

Guide words help you find words in the dictionary. They are the two words at the top of every dictionary page. Write the spelling word that would be on the same page as each pair of guide words.

9. off • only   10. fine • footstep

Word Analysis

1. _____
2. _____
3. _____
4. _____
5. _____

Sound and Letter Patterns

6. _____
7. _____
8. _____

Using the Dictionary

9. _____
10. _____

one	two	three	four	five
six	seven	eight	nine	ten

Complete the Sequences Write the spelling word that belongs in each group.

1. six, seven, _____
2. two, four, _____
3. six, five, _____
4. three, five, _____

Complete the Rhymes Write the spelling word that fits each clue. The spelling word will rhyme with the underlined word.

5. Who are those _____ boys?
6. I have to do just _____ more chore. Then I will be done.
7. That woman has _____ cats! She feels fine about it.
8. I might go to a summer camp when I am _____.
9. My friends saw _____ bees come out of that hive.
10. You must come see our _____ cute new puppies.

Complete the Sequences

1.
2.
3.
4.

Complete the Rhymes

5.
6.
7.
8.
9.
10.

Spelling and Writing

Proofread an Ad

Four words are not spelled correctly in this ad. Write the words correctly.

Roses for Sale

Buy rose plants cheap. They are big, lovely plants in big pots. Buy one plant for thre dollars or foor plants for tenn dollars! Pick from fiv kinds of roses.

Call 555-4537.

Ask for Victor. You will be glad you did.

Proofreading Marks

≡	Make a capital.
/	Make a small letter.
∧	Add something.
ℒ	Take out something.
⊙	Add a period.
⌗	New paragraph
SP	Spelling error

Write an Ad

Persuasive Writing

What might you sell? Write an ad for it. Be sure to tell

- what you are selling.
- how much it costs.
- why someone should buy it.

Use as many spelling words as you can.

Proofread Your Writing During

Writing Process

Prewriting
⇩
Drafting
⇩
Revising
⇩
Editing
⇩
Publishing

Proofread your writing for spelling errors as part of the editing stage in the writing process. Be sure to check each word carefully. Use a dictionary to check spelling if you are not sure.

Vocabulary

Preview Words: Number Words

Write the word from the box that fits each set of clues.

eighteen	fifteen	fifty-nine
sixteen	twenty-four	thirty-two

1. This number word ends in **teen**. It equals six plus ten.

2. This number word has both the **short i** and the **long i** sounds. It is the largest number listed.

3. This number word ends in **teen**. It equals eight plus ten.

4. This number word ends in **teen**. It is written with a one and a five.

5. This number word has three syllables and a **th** in its spelling.

6. This number word is made up of two words. It is written with a two and a four.

Preview Words

1. _____

2. _____

3. _____

4. _____

5. _____

6. _____

Connections

Content Words

Math: Numbers

Write the word from the box that can replace each underlined number or set of numbers.

twenty	fifty	thirty	sixty

1. I have <u>60</u> new trading cards for my collection.

2. There are <u>50</u> second-graders in our school.

3. My Aunt Sue is twelve years older than I am. She is <u>10 + 10</u> years old.

4. Today is my Uncle Bob's birthday. He is <u>10 + 10 + 10</u> years old.

Apply the Spelling Strategy

Circle the content word you wrote that has a **short e** sound.

Spelling and Thinking

end with -es

1. _____

2. _____

3. _____

4. _____

5. _____

end with -s

6. _____

7. _____

8. _____

9. _____

10. _____

READ THE SPELLING WORDS

1.	birds	The **birds** sing near my window.
2.	boxes	We fill two **boxes** with books.
3.	eggs	I fry two **eggs** for breakfast.
4.	glasses	Pam wears **glasses**.
5.	boats	Three **boats** are on the lake.
6.	dishes	The **dishes** are not clean.
7.	boys	Those **boys** are on my team.
8.	foxes	I saw two **foxes** in the woods.
9.	girls	The **girls** chat on the phone.
10.	wishes	My mom sends her best **wishes**.

SORT THE SPELLING WORDS

Words that mean "more than one" are called **plurals**.

1.–5. Write the spelling words that end with **-es**.

6.–10. Write the spelling words that end with **-s**.

REMEMBER THE SPELLING STRATEGY

Remember that words that show "more than one" often end in **-s** or **-es**: **boats, boxes**. These words are called **plurals**.

Spelling and Phonics

Rhyming Words

Write the spelling word that fits the sentence. The spelling word will rhyme with the underlined word.

1. The sailors put on their <u>coats</u> and got into their _____.

2. The happy _____ played with all their new <u>toys</u>.

3. I won two free <u>passes</u> to the movies. My mother won a set of new _____.

Word Building

Write spelling words by adding **-s** or **-es** to each word below.

4. egg
5. girl
6. fox
7. box
8. wish

A dictionary tells you the meanings of words. Write the spelling word for each dictionary meaning.

9. animals with feathers and wings

10. plates and other items for holding or serving food

Rhyming Words

1. _____

2. _____

3. _____

Word Building

4. _____

5. _____

6. _____

7. _____

8. _____

Using the Dictionary

9. _____

10. _____

Spelling and Reading

birds	boxes	eggs	glasses	boats
dishes	boys	foxes	girls	wishes

Complete the Sentences Write the spelling word that completes each sentence.

1. We buy fresh _____ from the chicken farm.
2. The boy in the story made three silent _____.

Complete the Paragraphs Write the spelling words that complete the paragraphs.

Moving day was a lot of work! Everyone needed to help out. I helped take some cardboard __3.__ off the van. The movers were very careful. We were all glad to hear that none of the __4.__ or __5.__ were broken. I am happy we packed them very carefully.

Moving makes me feel sad. I miss the __6.__ and __7.__ I used to play with. But I like the country. I am sure I will make new friends soon. There is a lake nearby where people sail in __8.__. I see so many __9.__ flying, too. I am going to make a feeder for them. I even saw two __10.__ in the woods. They have such bushy tails!

Complete the Sentences

1. _____
2. _____

Complete the Paragraphs

3. _____
4. _____
5. _____
6. _____
7. _____
8. _____
9. _____
10. _____

Spelling and Writing

Proofread a Paragraph

Four words are not spelled correctly in this paragraph. Write the words correctly.

My Wish

Today we hiked at Spring Hill. The girles spotted eleven kinds of birds. The boyes saw fourteen kinds of trees. I saw two red foxs near some berry bushes. We ate lunch near a cold, rocky stream.

If my wishs come true, I will go to Spring Hill again someday!

Proofreading Marks

≡ Make a capital.

/ Make a small letter.

∧ Add something.

℮ Take out something.

⊙ Add a period.

⌗ New paragraph

ⓢⓟ Spelling error

Write a Paragraph

Descriptive Writing

Think of a place you have visited. Tell what you saw there. Be sure to include

- the name of the place.
- what you saw there.
- words that tell color, size, shape, or other details.

Use as many spelling words as you can.

Writing Process

Prewriting
⇩
Drafting
⇩
Revising
⇩
Editing
⇩
Publishing

Proofread Your Writing During ➤ Editing

Proofread your writing for spelling errors as part of the editing stage in the writing process. Be sure to check each word carefully. Use a dictionary to check spelling if you are not sure.

Vocabulary

Strategy Words

Review Words

1. _____
2. _____
3. _____

Preview Words

4. _____
5. _____
6. _____

Review Words: Plurals -s, -es

Write the word from the box that fits each clue.

bug	cats	pants

1. This word names just one animal.
2. This word names something that is called a pair.
3. This word names more than one animal.

Preview Words: Plurals -s, -es

Write the word from the box that completes each sentence.

apples	benches	pies

4. City workers have put three new _____ in the park.
5. My mother and father bake peach _____ together.
6. Many _____ had fallen from the tree to the ground.

Connections

Content Words

Language Arts: Fairy Tales

Write words from the box to complete the story.

tall tale	footsteps	giant	bean

Once upon a time, a little girl planted a
___1.___. The bean plant grew and grew. It
grew right up into the clouds. One day the
little girl climbed the bean plant. When she
got to the top, she heard music and loud
___2.___. The sounds came from a huge
house. The girl peeked through a hole in the
door of the house. What do you think
she saw? She saw a ___3.___ dancing with
his giant dog!

Could this story be true? No! It is a ___4.___!

Apply the Spelling Strategy

Circle the content word you wrote that is plural.

Language Arts: Fairy Tales

1. _____

2. _____

3. _____

4. _____

-ed

1. _____

2. _____

3. _____

4. _____

5. _____

6. _____

-ing

7. _____

8. _____

9. _____

10. _____

Spelling and Thinking

READ THE SPELLING WORDS

1.	walked	We **walked** around the park.
2.	looking	I am **looking** at this book.
3.	planted	Ron **planted** peas and beans.
4.	asked	Jan **asked** a question.
5.	jumping	Rachel likes **jumping** rope.
6.	filled	I **filled** my glass to the top.
7.	talking	We are **talking** on the phone.
8.	needed	Pat **needed** to drink water.
9.	spelling	This **spelling** test is easy.
10.	played	Dan **played** checkers with me.

SORT THE SPELLING WORDS

1.–6. Write the spelling words that end with **-ed**.
Circle the **-ed** ending in each word.

7.–10. Write the spelling words that end with **-ing**.
Circle the **-ing** ending in each word.

REMEMBER THE SPELLING STRATEGY

Remember that you can add **-ed** and **-ing** to verbs
to make new words: **ask, asked, asking**.

Spelling and Phonics

Rhyming Words

Write the spelling word that fits each sentence. The spelling word will rhyme with the underlined word.

1. We <u>stayed</u> and ____ on the playground.
2. The flowers ____ some care, so Mr. Vacca <u>weeded</u> and watered them.
3. Ray has been <u>telling</u> me some ways to remember the ____ of words.
4. We ____ the <u>chilled</u> cups with fresh fruit.

Beginning Sounds

Write the spelling word that has the same beginning sound as each group of words.

5. jug, just, jungle, ____
6. wait, wash, water, ____
7. load, love, loop, ____

USING THE Dictionary

A dictionary tells you the meanings of words. Write the spelling word for each dictionary meaning.

8. tried to find out
9. put seeds in the ground to grow
10. saying; putting into speech

Rhyming Words

1. _____

2. _____

3. _____

4. _____

Beginning Sounds

5. _____

6. _____

7. _____

Using the Dictionary

8. _____

9. _____

10. _____

Spelling AND Reading

walked	looking	planted	asked	jumping
filled	talking	needed	spelling	played

Complete the Paragraph Write the spelling words that complete the paragraph.

Juanita went to the library. She wanted to borrow a book. She __1.__ out a form to get a library card. Then she __2.__ through the library. She was __3.__ for her favorite book. It was very quiet. Everyone was reading. No one was __4.__. The librarian __5.__ Juanita if she __6.__ help. Juanita said no. Soon she found her book.

Complete the Sentences Write the spelling word that completes each sentence.

7. An almanac can tell you who holds the record for ____ the highest.
8. A dictionary lets you check the ____ of a word.
9. Children's magazines can tell you how different games are ____.
10. Nonfiction books can give you information on how flowers are ____.

Complete the Paragraph

1. _____
2. _____
3. _____
4. _____
5. _____
6. _____

Complete the Sentences

7. _____
8. _____
9. _____
10. _____

Spelling and Writing

Proofread a Diary Entry

Four words are not spelled correctly in this diary entry. Write the words correctly.

Saturday

Dear Diary,

Today Dad needded me to help him plant a lilac bush. First we dug a hole. Then we plantied the bush and filled the hole with water and dirt. When we were done, we just stood lookking at our good work! Then we palyed catch.

Write a Diary Entry

Narrative Writing

Write a diary entry. Tell about your day yesterday or the day before. Be sure to
- tell who was there and what you did.
- write down details you want to remember.

Use as many spelling words as you can.

Writing Process

Prewriting
⇩
Drafting
⇩
Revising
⇩
Proofread Your Writing During ▶ Editing
⇩
Publishing

Proofread your writing for spelling errors as part of the editing stage in the writing process. Be sure to check each word carefully. Use a dictionary to check spelling if you are not sure.

Vocabulary

Strategy Words

Review Words

1. _____

2. _____

3. _____

Preview Words

4. _____

5. _____

6. _____

Review Words: Endings -ed, -ing

Write the word from the box that best takes the place of the underlined word or words.

packed	packing	picked

1. Max is <u>putting clothes into his suitcase</u> for a trip to Grandma's house.
2. Each crate was <u>stuffed</u> with fresh fruit.
3. Mary Ellen <u>chose</u> me to be the first batter.

Preview Words: Endings -ed, -ing

Write the word from the box that fits each clue.

dashed	fishing	sleeping

4. It begins like **day** and ends like **wished**.
5. It rhymes with **keeping**.
6. It has the **short i** sound.

Connections

Content Words

Health: Games

Write words from the box that complete the paragraph.

race	winner	team	won

    Bob, Nora, and Evan formed a __1.__. They wanted to be in the relay __2.__ at school. They practiced running every day for two weeks. They hoped their team would be the __3.__. On the day of the race, they ran fast and hard. Their team __4.__! Bob, Nora, and Evan are proud of their trophy.

Apply the Spelling Strategy

Circle the content word that is used to make the word **raced**.

Health: Games

1. _____

2. _____

3. _____

4. _____

long oo

1. _____

2. _____

3. _____

4. _____

5. _____

short oo

6. _____

7. _____

8. _____

9. _____

10. _____

Spelling and Thinking

READ THE SPELLING WORDS

1. wood	The desk is made of **wood**.
2. took	Len **took** a bus to the game.
3. too	It is **too** cold for swimming.
4. noon	We eat lunch at **noon**.
5. good	I feel **good** after a nap.
6. root	A **root** grows underground.
7. book	This **book** tells about caves.
8. boot	That **boot** has a large heel.
9. wool	Is the vest made of **wool**?
10. food	We pack **food** for our trip.

SORT THE SPELLING WORDS

1.–5. Write the spelling words that have the **long oo** sound. Circle the letters that spell this sound in each word.

6.–10. Write the spelling words that have the **short oo** sound. Circle the letters that spell this sound in each word.

REMEMBER THE SPELLING STRATEGY

Remember that you can hear the **short oo** sound in **wood**. You can hear the **long oo** sound in **boot**.

Spelling ^an_d Phonics

Word Analysis

Write the spelling word that fits each clue.

1. This word sounds the same as **two**.
2. This word sounds the same as **would**.
3. This word is the same spelled forward or backward.
4. This word rhymes with **cook** and begins like **top**.

Sound and Letter Patterns

These spelling words are missing letters.
Write the spelling words.

5. g __ __ d
7. f __ __ d
9. b __ __ k

6. w __ __ l
8. b __ __ t

USING THE Dictionary

An **entry word** in the dictionary may have more than one meaning.

10. Write the spelling word with these meanings.
    - part of a plant
    - to dig up
    - to cheer for

Spelling and Reading

wood	took	too	noon	good
root	book	boot	wool	food

Complete the Paragraph

1. _____
2. _____
3. _____
4. _____
5. _____
6. _____
7. _____
8. _____

Solve the Analogies

9. _____
10. _____

Complete the Paragraph Write the spelling words that complete the paragraph.

Everything comes from something or somewhere. Trees give us many of the things we use. A __1.__ is made from paper. Some paper is made from the __2.__ of trees. Tables and chairs are made from wood, __3.__. Some important things come from animals. We use __4.__ from sheep to make clothes, blankets, and rugs. A __5.__ can be made from rubber, leather, or heavy cloth. Did you know that some of our __6.__ comes from under the ground? A vegetable that grows in the ground is called a __7.__. Carrots are roots. They are __8.__ to eat. They give us what we need to grow and stay healthy.

Solve the Analogies Write a spelling word to complete each analogy.

9. **Breakfast** is to **morning** as **lunch** is to _____.
10. **Give** is to **gave** as **take** is to _____.

Spelling and Writing

Proofread a Letter

Four words are not spelled correctly in this letter. Write the words correctly.

Dear Grace,

   A bus tuke our class to Pine Farm. We saw wull cut from sheep. We learned about rout vegetables and other crops. We had a good time. We were back by nune.

                    Your pal,
                    Sean

Proofreading Marks

≡ Make a capital.
/ Make a small letter.
∧ Add something.
℣ Take out something.
⊙ Add a period.
⌗ New paragraph
ⓢⓟ Spelling error

Write a Letter

Narrative Writing

Think of something fun you did. Write a letter to a friend about it. Don't forget to

- begin your letter with **Dear**.
- place commas after your greeting and after your closing.
- indent your paragraphs, your closing, and your signature.

Use as many spelling words as you can.

Proofread Your Writing During ➤ **Editing**

Writing Process

Prewriting
⬇
Drafting
⬇
Revising
⬇
Editing
⬇
Publishing

Proofread your writing for spelling errors as part of the editing stage in the writing process. Be sure to check each word carefully. Use a dictionary to check spelling if you are not sure.

Vocabulary

Strategy Words

Review Words

1. _____

2. _____

3. _____

Preview Words

4. _____

5. _____

6. _____

Review Words: Long and Short oo

Replace the underlined letters to write a word from the box.

moon	room	soon

1. so**il**   2. m**oa**n   3. **b**oom

Preview Words: Long and Short oo

Write the word from the box that best takes the place of the underlined word or words.

barefoot	choose	goose

4. You can <u>pick</u> any new baseball glove you want.

5. We walked <u>without shoes</u> along the beach.

6. We saw the <u>large bird</u> near the edge of the pond.

Connections

Content Words

Language Arts: Onomatopoeia

Write the word from the box that completes each sentence.

moo	roar	chirp	squeak

1. I hear the birds _____ early in the morning.
2. A mouse will _____ when it is afraid.
3. Did you hear the loud _____ of the lion at the zoo?
4. The farmer's cows always _____ when they see me coming.

Apply the Spelling Strategy

Circle the letters that spell the **long oo** sound in one of the content words you wrote.

Language Arts: Onomatopoeia

1. _____

2. _____

3. _____

4. _____

Unit 19

1. _____

2. _____

3. _____

Unit 21

4. _____

5. _____

Unit 22

6. _____

7. _____

Unit 23

8. _____

9. _____

10. _____

Assessment and Review

Assessment Units 19–23

Each Assessment Word in the box fits one of the spelling strategies you have studied over the past five weeks. Read the spelling strategies. Then write each Assessment Word under the unit number it fits. You will not write any words for Unit 20.

Unit 19 _____

1.–3. Consonant clusters with **l** and **r** are heard at the beginning of the words **fly** and **free**.

Unit 20 _____

There is a word name for each number. It is important to spell number words correctly.

Unit 21 _____

4.–5. Words that show "more than one" often end in **-s** or **-es: boats, boxes**. These words are called **plurals**.

Unit 22 _____

6.–7. You can add **-ed** and **-ing** to verbs to make new words: **ask, asked, asking**.

Unit 23 _____

8.–10. You can hear the **short oo** sound in **wood**. You can hear the **long oo** sound in **boot**.

hook

looked

days

sly

hood

being

weeks

frame

graze

stoop

Review Unit 19: Consonant Clusters

slow	train	please	drive	tree

Write a spelling word by adding a letter before each word.

1. rain   **2.** low

Write the spelling word that rhymes with each word.

3. strive   **4.** sneeze   **5.** free

Review Unit 20: Number Words

one	four	two	eight	three

Write a spelling word for each clue.

6. This word has the /**w**/ sound, but no **w**. It is the first number you use when you count.

7. This word sounds like **to**. It names the number of things in a pair.

8. This word begins like **throw** and ends like **see**. It names the number of wheels on a tricycle.

Write a spelling word that fits each shape.

9.   **10.**

Unit 19

1. _____

2. _____

3. _____

4. _____

5. _____

Unit 20

6. _____

7. _____

8. _____

9. _____

10. _____

147

Unit 21

1.

2.

3.

4.

5.

Unit 22

6.

7.

8.

9.

10.

 **Unit 21: Plurals -s, -es**

| girls | boxes | boys | dishes | birds |

Write spelling words by adding **-s** or **-es**.

1. dish   **2.** box   **3.** boy

Write the spelling word that fits each shape.

4.   **5.**

Review **Unit 22: Endings -ed, -ing**

| asked | needed | played | looking | talking |

Write the spelling word that completes each sentence.

6. Yesterday afternoon we _____ soccer in the field at the park.

7. Mom said we _____ to go home and eat dinner at 5:00.

8. Joe _____ if we could please play until 5:30.

Write the spelling word that fits each shape.

9. **10.**

good	too	took	noon	food

Write the spelling word that completes each sentence.
The spelling word will rhyme with the underlined word.

1. <u>Soon</u> it will be _____.

2. I am in the <u>mood</u> for some tasty _____.

3. Did you happen to find any _____, dry <u>wood</u>?

4. Jamie just _____ the big fish off the <u>hook</u>.

5. Is this what <u>you</u> want, _____?

Unit 23

1. _____

2. _____

3. _____

4. _____

5. _____

 **Spelling Study Strategy**

Sorting by Sounds

You can practice spelling words by placing them into groups. Here is one way to do that.

1. Make three columns on a piece of paper. Label one column **Short Vowels**. Label the next column **Long Vowels** and the last column **Other**.

2. With a partner, take turns finding spelling words to write in each column. Write the words.

3. Say the words aloud and check the spelling of each word.

Grammar, Usage, and Mechanics

Nouns

A noun names a person, place, or thing. A common noun names any person, place, or thing.

The **student** went to that **state** and saw a **fort**.

A proper noun names a certain person, place, or thing. Proper nouns begin with a capital letter.

Sally went to **Texas** and saw the **Alamo**.

Practice Activity

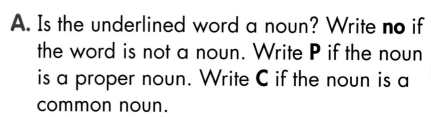

A. Is the underlined word a noun? Write **no** if the word is not a noun. Write **P** if the noun is a proper noun. Write **C** if the noun is a common noun.

1. Juan <u>walked</u> here.
2. I took the <u>train</u>.
3. Did <u>Tina</u> go slow?
4. Let's go to <u>Mexico</u>!
5. I like <u>yellow</u> flowers.

B. Complete each sentence with a noun from the box. Write the word.

tree	sing	dishes	drop	boxes

6. Put the forks next to the _____.
7. Put the crayons back in the _____.
8. An oak _____ shades our house.

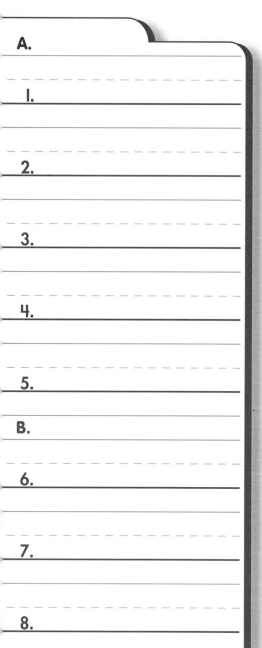

A.

1.

2.

3.

4.

5.

B.

6.

7.

8.

WORKSHOP

Read Backwards

Good writers always proofread their writing for spelling mistakes. Here's a strategy you can use to proofread your papers.

Instead of reading your paper from the first word to the last word, try reading it backwards. Read it from the last word to the first. So you would read the sentence **The computer was brand new** like this: **new brand was computer The**.

E-Mail

Using e-mail is a fast way to write to people worldwide.

But your e-mail will not arrive if you do not address it correctly. E-mail addresses must have three parts: a user name, the symbol @, and a domain name. The domain name often ends with a period (called a **dot**) followed by **com, edu, org,** or **gov**.

Which addresses are missing parts or letters? Write **OK** if the address is OK and **wrong** if it is not.

1. kids@city.com   **2.** beth@amol.cm

3. seth@forgov   **4.** reggie@shows.org

5. staci2utext.edu   **6.** sam@zephyr.orig

Electronic Spelling

1.
2.
3.
4.
5.
6.

one syllable

_____
1. _____
_____
2. _____
_____
3. _____
_____
4. _____
_____
5. _____
_____
6. _____
_____
7. _____
_____
8. _____

two syllables

_____
9. _____
_____
10. _____

Spelling and Thinking

READ THE SPELLING WORDS

1.	put	I **put** the key in the lock.
2.	want	Do you **want** a new bike?
3.	many	Paul asked **many** questions.
4.	out	The sign says, "Keep **out**."
5.	saw	I **saw** a deer cross the road.
6.	who	Ed is the one **who** read last.
7.	off	Please stay **off** the roof.
8.	any	Do you have **any** money left?
9.	from	This letter is **from** Sylvia.
10.	her	Amanda lost **her** book.

SORT THE SPELLING WORDS

1.–8. Write the spelling words that have one syllable.

9.–10. Write the spelling words that have two syllables.

REMEMBER THE SPELLING STRATEGY

Remember that it is important to spell words correctly that you use often in writing.

Word Analysis

Write a spelling word that matches each clue.

1. It begins with a **short e** sound spelled **a**.
2. It has the vowel sound in **ball** and a double consonant.
3. It rhymes with **to**.
4. It has a **short u** sound spelled with **o**.
5. It rhymes with **shout**.

Sound and Letter Patterns

Write the spelling word that fits each clue.

6. This word begins like **help** and ends like **far**.
7. This word begins like **pup** and ends like **boot**.
8. This word begins like **wash** and ends like **dent**.
9. This word begins like **made** and ends like **funny**.

10. Write the spelling word that has these meanings:
   • a tool or machine used for cutting
   • the past tense of **see**

◆ ◆ ◆

Dictionary Check Be sure to check the meanings in your **Spelling Dictionary**.

Word Analysis

1. _____

2. _____

3. _____

4. _____

5. _____

Sound and Letter Patterns

6. _____

7. _____

8. _____

9. _____

Using the Dictionary

10. _____

put	want	many	out	saw
who	off	any	from	her

Solve the Analogies

Solve the Analogies Write a spelling word to complete each analogy.

1. **Food** is to **bread** as **tool** is to _____.
2. **Sometimes** is to **some** as **anymore** is to _____.
3. **Help** is to **aid** as **wish** is to _____.
4. **He** is to **his** as **she** is to _____.
5. **Send** is to **receive** as **to** is to _____.

Complete the Paragraph Write the spelling words that complete the paragraph.

The Story of Earmuffs

Do you know __6.__ invented earmuffs? Chester Greenwood invented them in 1873. He was fifteen years old. First he made loops __7.__ of wire. His grandmother __8.__ fur and velvet on them. Then Chester hooked the loops to his cap. Today, you see __9.__ people wearing earmuffs to keep their ears warm. "Hats __10.__"
to Chester Greenwood!

Solve the Analogies

1. _____
2. _____
3. _____
4. _____
5. _____

Complete the Paragraph

6. _____
7. _____
8. _____
9. _____
10. _____

Spelling and Writing

Proofread a Poster

Four words are not spelled correctly in this poster. Write the words correctly.

> ### USED TOY SALE
>
> Saturday, June 4, 10 A.M. to noon
> Tammy DiLuca's house, 10 Maple Street
>
> Do you wont more toys? I will have meny toys for sale. Choose frum dolls, games, balls, and kites. Be there at 10 when I put them owt!

Proofreading Marks

≡ Make a capital.

/ Make a small letter.

∧ Add something.

℮ Take out something.

⊙ Add a period.

⌗ New paragraph

(SP) Spelling error

Write a Poster

Persuasive Writing

Write a poster for a yard sale or another event. Be sure to tell

- the time and place.
- what will happen.
- why people should come.

Use as many spelling words as you can.

Writing Process

Prewriting
⇩
Drafting
⇩
Revising
⇩
Editing
⇩
Publishing

Proofread Your Writing During ➤ Editing

Proofread your writing for spelling errors as part of the editing stage in the writing process. Be sure to check each word carefully. Use a dictionary to check spelling if you are not sure.

Vocabulary

Strategy Words

Review Words
1. _____
2. _____
3. _____

Preview Words
4. _____
5. _____
6. _____

Review Words: Words Writers Use

Write the word from the box that completes each sentence. This word will rhyme with the underlined word.

name	was	we

1. Where are _____ supposed to be?
2. Did you learn the _____ of the game?
3. Does anyone know what that animal _____?

Preview Words: Words Writers Use

Write the word from the box that fits each clue.

away	busy	real

4. It means the opposite of "doing nothing."
5. It is the opposite of **fake**.
6. It can mean "out of the house." It can also name a sporting event that is not played at home.

Connections

Content Words

Science: Animals

Write the word from the box that completes each sentence.

| lion | donkey | tiger | monkey |

1. The _____ is sometimes called the "king of the jungle."
2. An animal that has hands like a person is a _____.
3. A _____ has orange fur with black stripes.
4. An animal that is in the horse family is the _____.

Apply the Spelling Strategy

Circle the letters that spell the **long i** sound in two of the content words you wrote.

Science: Animals

1. _____

2. _____

3. _____

4. _____

Spelling and Thinking

ow

1. _____
2. _____
3. _____
4. _____
5. _____
6. _____

ew

7. _____
8. _____
9. _____
10. _____

READ THE SPELLING WORDS

1.	how	I know **how** to ride a bike.
2.	new	I just bought this **new** dress.
3.	cow	A **cow** gives milk.
4.	clown	The **clown** makes us laugh.
5.	blew	We **blew** bubbles in the park.
6.	town	Our **town** has one post office.
7.	flew	The birds **flew** south.
8.	now	We must leave the house **now**.
9.	grew	The rose **grew** in my garden.
10.	down	Go **down** the stairs.

SORT THE SPELLING WORDS

1.–6. Write the spelling words with the letters **ow**.

7.–10. Write the spelling words with the letters **ew**.

REMEMBER THE SPELLING STRATEGY

Remember that the **long oo** sound in **new** can be spelled with the vowel digraph **ew**. The vowel sound in **cow** can be spelled with the vowel digraph **ow**.

Sound and Letter Patterns

Write the spelling words by adding the missing letters.

1. bl __ __

2. h __ __

Beginning Sounds

Write the spelling word that completes each sentence. The spelling word will have the same beginning sound as the underlined word.

3. These <u>great</u> carrots ____ in our garden.

4. <u>Today</u> is the day our ____ will have a parade.

5. The butterflies ____ near the <u>flowers</u>.

6. Did you see that <u>dog</u> go ____ the stairs?

USING THE Dictionary

The words in a dictionary are in a-b-c order.

7.–10. Write these spelling words in a-b-c order.

now   clown   new   cow

◆ ◆ ◆

Dictionary Check Be sure to check the a-b-c order of the words in your **Spelling Dictionary**.

Sound and Letter Patterns

1.

2.

Beginning Sounds

3.

4.

5.

6.

Using the Dictionary

7.

8.

9.

10.

Spelling and Reading

how	new	cow	clown	blew
town	flew	now	grew	down

Complete the Sequences
Write the spelling word that tells what comes next.

1. one home, group of homes, many groups of homes, _____

2. an hour ago, a minute ago, _____

Solve the Analogies
Write a spelling word to complete each analogy.

3. **Zoo** is to **polar bear** as **circus** is to _____.

4. **High** is to **low** as **up** is to _____.

5. **Forest** is to **deer** as **farm** is to _____.

6. **Narrow** is to **wide** as **old** is to _____.

7. **Map** is to **where** as **directions** are to _____.

Change the Time
Write the spelling word that completes the meaning. The word you write will name the past tense form of the underlined word.

8. I love to <u>fly</u> in an airplane. Last year I _____ to another state.

9. The winds <u>blow</u> hard and cold in winter. Last winter they _____ the roof off my birdhouse.

10. Sunflowers <u>grow</u> in our yard. One sunflower _____ six feet tall last summer.

Spelling and Writing

Proofread a Paragraph

Four words are not spelled correctly in this paragraph. Write the words correctly.

One day Pouncer hurt his leg. I do not know how he did it. Maybe he fell doawn. I took him to the vet in my toun. She put Pouncer's leg in a splint. Pouncer is all better nou. In fact, he acts like a brand neuw cat!

Proofreading Marks

≡ Make a capital.

/ Make a small letter.

∧ Add something.

℮ Take out something.

⊙ Add a period.

New paragraph

SP Spelling error

Write a Paragraph

Narrative Writing

Think of something that happened to you, to a friend, or to a pet. Write about it. Be sure to tell
- who was there.
- what happened.

Use as many spelling words as you can.

Writing Process

Prewriting
⇩
Drafting
⇩
Revising
⇩
Proofread Your Writing During ➤ Editing
⇩
Publishing

Proofread your writing for spelling errors as part of the editing stage in the writing process. Be sure to check each word carefully. Use a dictionary to check spelling if you are not sure.

Vocabulary

Strategy Words

Review Words

1. _____

2. _____

3. _____

Preview Words

4. _____

5. _____

6. _____

Review Words: Vowel Digraphs ew, ow

Write the word from the box that fits each clue.

do	to	you

1. This word begins like **dog**. Its vowel sound is spelled like the vowel sound in **who**.
2. This word spells its vowel sound with two vowel letters.
3. This word begins like **take**.

Preview Words: Vowel Digraphs ew, ow

Write the word from the box that completes each sentence and rhymes with the underlined word.

chew	drew	towns

4. Jen _____ a picture of <u>dew</u> on a leaf.
5. Max used reds and <u>browns</u> to paint his picture of the _____.
6. Did the puppy _____ my <u>new</u> shoe?

Connections

Content Words

Science: Gardening

Write the word from the box that matches each meaning.

garden	bulb	sprout	hoe

1. a tool used to break up soil
2. a round plant part that grows under the ground
3. to begin to grow
4. a place where things are planted and grow

Apply the Spelling Strategy

Circle the content word you wrote that has the vowel sound you hear in **cow**.

Science: Gardening

1. _____

2. _____

3. _____

4. _____

one syllable

1. _____

2. _____

3. _____

4. _____

5. _____

6. _____

7. _____

8. _____

two syllables

9. _____

10. _____

Spelling and Thinking

READ THE SPELLING WORDS

1. red   A stop sign is **red**.
2. blue   The sky is **blue** today.
3. yellow   We painted the room **yellow**.
4. gray   A **gray** sky can mean rain.
5. brown   The fallen leaves turn **brown**.
6. color   What **color** is your new bike?
7. black   Burned paper is **black**.
8. green   That grass looks so **green**!
9. pink   Here are two **pink** roses for you.
10. white   The snow is cold and **white**.

SORT THE SPELLING WORDS

1.–8. Write the spelling words that have one syllable.

9.–10. Write the spelling words that have two syllables.

REMEMBER THE SPELLING STRATEGY

Remember that each color has a name. It is important to spell color words correctly.

Spelling and Phonics

Beginning and Ending Sounds

1. Write the spelling word that ends with the /**k**/ sound spelled **ck**.

2. Write the spelling word that ends with the **long o** sound spelled **ow**.

3. Write the spelling word that begins like **what** and rhymes with **kite**.

4. Write the spelling word that rhymes with **bed** and begins like **rock**.

Sound and Letter Patterns

Write the spelling words by adding the missing letters.

5. c __ l __ r   6. pi __ __

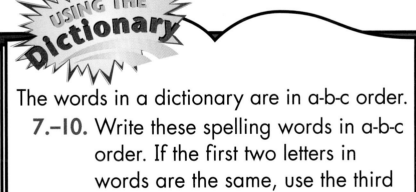

USING THE Dictionary

The words in a dictionary are in a-b-c order.

7.–10. Write these spelling words in a-b-c order. If the first two letters in words are the same, use the third letter to put them in a-b-c order.

gray   green   brown   blue

red   blue   yellow   gray   brown

color   black   green   pink   white

Answer the Riddles   Write the spelling word that answers each riddle.

1. I am the color of mice. I am the color of the sky on a day that is not nice. What color am I?

2. I am the color of a polar bear. I am the color of the inside of a pear. What color am I?

3. I am the color of the sky at night. I am the color of a room when there is no light. What color am I?

Complete the Paragraphs   Write spelling words to complete the paragraphs.

At a stoplight, a bike rider must obey the __4.__ of the light. If the light is __5.__, it is all right to go ahead. If it is __6.__, get ready to stop. If it is __7.__, stop.

You can make new colors by mixing several colors together. Red and white mixed together make __8.__. You can mix yellow and __9.__ to get green. By mixing many colors, you can get black or __10.__.

Answer the Riddles

1. _____

2. _____

3. _____

Complete the Paragraphs

4. _____

5. _____

6. _____

7. _____

8. _____

9. _____

10. _____

Spelling and Writing

Proofread a Paragraph

Four words are not spelled correctly in this paragraph. Write the words correctly.

Flags have different colors and designs.

 Our country's flag has red and wite stripes.

It has stars on a background of bleu. The

 flag of Vietnam is red with a big yello star.

 The flags of Ireland and India have bands

 of grene and orange.

Proofreading Marks	
≡	Make a capital.
/	Make a small letter.
∧	Add something.
℘	Take out something.
⊙	Add a period.
♯	New paragraph
SP	Spelling error

Write a Paragraph
Expository Writing

What facts do you know about colors? Write a paragraph that gives information about just one subject. You might tell about the colors of insects, leaves, or clothing. Be sure to

• write a sentence at the beginning of your paragraph that tells what your writing is about.

• give facts.

Use as many spelling words as you can.

Writing Process

Prewriting
⇩
Drafting
⇩
Revising
⇩
Editing
⇩
Publishing

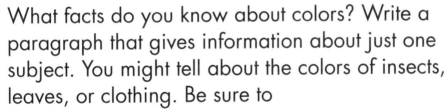
Proofread Your Writing During Editing

Proofread your writing for spelling errors as part of the editing stage in the writing process. Be sure to check each word carefully. Use a dictionary to check spelling if you are not sure.

Vocabulary

Unit 27 enrichment

Strategy Words

Review Words

1. _____

2. _____

3. _____

Preview Words

4. _____

5. _____

6. _____

Review Words: Color Words

Write a word from the box to complete each sentence.

pig	pot	ship

1. The bottom of the old ____ is black.
2. The skin of a ____ is pink in color.
3. We could see only the gray sides of the ____ on the water.

Preview Words: Color Words

Write the word from the box that fits each clue.

rainbow	redder	greenhouse

4. This word is made up of two words. One of the two words names a color.
5. This word is made up of two words. It names something with many colors.
6. This word can come between **red** and **reddest**.

168

Connections

Content Words

Science: Bugs

Write the word from the box that matches each meaning.

butterfly	spider	cocoon	web

1. a case made of silky strands that holds some kinds of insects in their early stage of life
2. silky strands woven by a spider and used to trap insects
3. small animal with eight legs
4. flying insect with large wings and a narrow body

Apply the Spelling Strategy

Circle the content word you wrote that names a colorful insect.

Science: Bugs

1. _____
2. _____
3. _____
4. _____

Spelling and Thinking

rhyme with bar

1. _____

2. _____

3. _____

rhyme with harm

4. _____

5. _____

rhyme with cart

6. _____

7. _____

rhyme with bark

8. _____

9. _____

rhymes with card

10. _____

READ THE SPELLING WORDS

1. far   My house is not **far** from here.

2. farm   We saw cows at the **farm**.

3. art   I draw and paint in **art** class.

4. park   Mom can **park** the van here.

5. car   His **car** had a flat tire.

6. part   A switch is **part** of a light.

7. dark   I cannot see you in the **dark**.

8. star   Look at that **star** in the sky.

9. hard   Old bread gets stale and **hard**.

10. arm   My **arm** is tired from throwing.

SORT THE SPELLING WORDS

1.–3. Write the spelling words that rhyme with **bar**.

4.–5. Write the spelling words that rhyme with **harm**.

6.–7. Write the spelling words that rhyme with **cart**.

8.–9. Write the spelling words that rhyme with **bark**.

10. Write the spelling word that rhymes with **card**.

REMEMBER THE SPELLING STRATEGY

Remember that the /är/ vowel sound you hear in **car** can be spelled **ar**.

Spelling and Phonics

Word Structure

Replace the underlined letters to make a spelling word.

1. f<u>ur</u>

2. pa<u>c</u>k

3. st<u>ep</u>

4. p<u>in</u>t

Rhyming Words

Write a spelling word that fits the sentence. The spelling word will rhyme with the underlined word.

5. It was _____ to find the right <u>card</u> to send to my Uncle Tyrone.

6. I found a <u>charm</u> on the ground at the _____.

7. I am going to <u>start</u> a new painting in _____ class next week.

8. My dog will <u>bark</u> at anyone who comes to our house in the _____.

USING THE Dictionary

Write the spelling words that would be found between these guide words.

9. brown • clam   **10.** add • bean

◆ ◆ ◆

Dictionary Check Be sure to check the guide words in your **Spelling Dictionary**.

Word Structure

1. _____

2. _____

3. _____

4. _____

Rhyming Words

5. _____

6. _____

7. _____

8. _____

Using the Dictionary

9. _____

10. _____

far	farm	art	park	car
part	dark	star	hard	arm

Complete the Paragraph

Complete the Paragraph Write spelling words to complete the paragraph.

Anna Mary Robertson, known as Grandma Moses, was a famous painter. Grandma Moses was born on a __1.__. As a child, she worked __2.__. She also spent __3.__ of her time picking wildflowers. Most of her paintings were done after she was seventy years old. Many of her paintings showed pictures of life in the country. In 1940, her paintings were seen at an __4.__ show. Soon Grandma Moses became very famous. Her paintings were admired by thousands. Today people come from near and __5.__ to see her work.

Solve the Analogies

Solve the Analogies Write a spelling word to complete each analogy.

6. **Pilot** is to **plane** as **driver** is to ____.
7. **Foot** is to **leg** as **hand** is to ____.
8. **Shine** is to **sun** as **twinkle** is to ____.
9. **Plane** is to **land** as **car** is to ____.
10. **Day** is to **night** as **light** is to ____.

Complete the Paragraph

1. _____
2. _____
3. _____
4. _____
5. _____

Solve the Analogies

6. _____
7. _____
8. _____
9. _____
10. _____

Spelling and Writing

Proofread a Poem

Four words are not spelled correctly in this poem. Write the words correctly.

> By the light of a star
>
> So farr away,
>
> I wonder how this daerk world
>
> turns into day.
>
> I ask myself what parrt
>
> the moon and stars play
>
> in the nighttime airt
>
> of taking blackness away.

Proofreading Marks

≡ Make a capital.

/ Make a small letter.

∧ Add something.

ℓ Take out something.

⊙ Add a period.

New paragraph

SP Spelling error

Write a Poem

Descriptive Writing

Write a poem about something that surprises you or makes you wonder. Begin with something you can see. The lines of your poem do not have to rhyme. Be sure to

- tell what you see.
- tell what about it makes you think or wonder.

Use as many spelling words as you can.

Writing Process

Prewriting
⇩
Drafting
⇩
Revising
⇩
Proofread Your Writing During ⯈ Editing
⇩
Publishing

Proofread your writing for spelling errors as part of the editing stage in the writing process. Be sure to check each word carefully. Use a dictionary to check spelling if you are not sure.

Vocabulary

Strategy Words

Review Words

1. _____

2. _____

3. _____

Preview Words

4. _____

5. _____

6. _____

Review Words: r-Controlled a Spelled ar

Write the word from the box for each clue.

are	card	cards

1. This word begins with the /**k**/ sound spelled **c** and names more than one.

2. This word begins like **can** and rhymes with **hard**.

3. was, were; is, _____

Preview Words: r-Controlled a Spelled ar

Write the word from the box that fits each clue.

starfish	shark	faraway

4. It is a large fish with sharp teeth.

5. It is the opposite of **near**.

6. It is a sea animal with five parts that are like arms.

Connections

Content Words

Social Studies: Independence Day

Write words from the box to complete the paragraph.

flag	stripes	stars	parade

Have you ever watched a __1.__ on the Fourth of July? If you have, you probably saw the American __2.__. It is sometimes called the "Stars and Stripes." It has thirteen __3.__. Seven are red, and six are white. The flag also has white __4.__. Do you know what the stars stand for? (Here is a hint. There are fifty stars.)

Apply the Spelling Strategy

Circle the letters that spell the /är/ sound in one of the content words you wrote.

Social Studies: Independence Day

1. _____

2. _____

3. _____

4. _____

wh and ch

1.

wh

2.

3.

4.

5.

ch

6.

7.

8.

9.

10.

Spelling and Thinking

READ THE SPELLING WORDS

1. chop   We **chop** onions for the stew.
2. each   I gave one bag to **each** child.
3. when   Six o'clock is **when** we eat.
4. chin   The **chin** is part of the face.
5. what   Please find out **what** Jeff wants.
6. such   This is **such** windy weather.
7. why   I don't know **why** Sam did that.
8. much   How **much** does that hat cost?
9. while   I water **while** Fran weeds.
10. which   **Which** one is mine?

SORT THE SPELLING WORDS

1. Write the word that is spelled with both **wh** and **ch**.

2.–5. Write the other words that are spelled with **wh**.

6.–10. Write the other words that are spelled with **ch**.

REMEMBER THE SPELLING STRATEGY

Remember that the **wh** digraph you hear at the beginning of **which** is spelled **wh**. The digraph you hear at the end of **which** is spelled **ch**.

Spelling and Phonics

Sound and Letter Patterns —·—·—·—·

Write a spelling word to fit each clue.

1. This word has the **long i** sound spelled **i-consonant-e**. It rhymes with **mile**.

2. This word begins with the **long e** sound spelled **ea**. It rhymes with **beach**.

3. This word has the **long i** sound spelled **y**. It rhymes with **fly**.

Word Structure —————————

Replace the underlined letters to write a spelling word.

4. s<u>h</u>in   5. m<u>a</u>th

6. su<u>ng</u>   7. <u>sh</u>ip

The words in a dictionary are in a-b-c order.

8.–10. Write these words in a-b-c order.

     which   when   what

◆ ◆ ◆

Dictionary Check Be sure to check the a-b-c order of the words in your **Spelling Dictionary**.

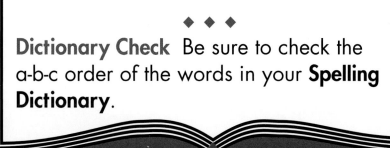

Sound and Letter Patterns

1. _____

2. _____

3. _____

Word Structure

4. _____

5. _____

6. _____

7. _____

Using the Dictionary

8. _____

9. _____

10. _____

Spelling and Reading

chop	each	when	chin	what
such	why	much	while	which

Complete the Sentences

1.

2.

3.

4.

5.

6.

7.

Replace the Words

8.

9.

10.

Complete the Sentences Write the spelling word that completes each sentence.

1. The forest ranger said hello to _____ of us.

2. He had a smile on his face and a big beard on his _____.

3. Some rangers meet with groups like ours, _____ others stay in the forest.

4. He spoke to us about _____ forest rangers do to protect the trees and animals.

5. They must be on the lookout for fires, _____ are not always easy to find.

6. There is so _____ work in the forest that rangers are always busy.

7. There are books about forest rangers, _____ as What Does a Forest Ranger Do?

Replace the Words Write the spelling word that could best take the place of the underlined word or words.

8. It can be sad to see people <u>cut</u> down trees.

9. Do you know <u>at what time</u> Ana will come to the meeting?

10. I did not learn <u>for what reason</u> we could not go to the park.

Spelling  and Writing

Proofread Interview Questions

Four words are not spelled correctly in this list of questions for an interview. Write the words correctly.

> Hwat is your job?
>
> Which part of your job do you like best?
>
> Wen did you know you wanted that job?
>
> Whi did you choose that kind of work?
>
> How musch time do you spend at work
>
>   each day?

Write Interview Questions — Expository Writing

Think of an adult you could interview. Write a list of questions to ask about the work this person does. Be sure to write questions

- that will give you all the important facts.
- in an order that makes sense.

Use as many spelling words as you can.

Writing Process

Prewriting

⇩

Drafting

⇩

Revising

⇩

Proofread Your Writing During ▶ Editing

⇩

Publishing

Proofread your writing for spelling errors as part of the editing stage in the writing process. Be sure to check each word carefully. Use a dictionary to check spelling if you are not sure.

Vocabulary

Strategy Words

Review Words

1. _____
2. _____
3. _____

Preview Words

4. _____
5. _____
6. _____

Review Words: ch, wh

Write the word from the box that belongs in each group.

cheek	chips	wheel

1. popcorn, crackers, _____
2. seat, frame, handlebars, _____
3. ear, eye, _____

Preview Words: ch, wh

Write the word from the box that fits each clue.

chain	lunch	whale

4. It is a very large sea animal.
5. It comes between breakfast and dinner.
6. It can be small enough to go around your neck or big enough to hold a ship in place.

Connections

Content Words

Social Studies: Farming

Write words from the box to complete the paragraph.

grain	silo	hay	wheat

Grain comes from plants like corn, __1.__, and rice. If you have ever eaten cereal, then you have eaten __2.__. Farm animals, like horses and cows, eat grain, too. They also eat __3.__. Farmers store hay in a hayloft. They store grain in a tall, round building called a __4.__. Can you think of other foods you eat that come from a farm?

Apply the Spelling Strategy

Circle the **wh** digraph in one of the content words you wrote.

Social Studies: Farming

1.

2.

3.

4.

Unit 26

1. _____

2. _____

3. _____

Unit 28

4. _____

5. _____

6. _____

Unit 29

7. _____

8. _____

9. _____

10. _____

Assessment and Review

Assessment — Units 25–29

Each Assessment Word in the box fits one of the spelling strategies you have studied over the past five weeks. Read the spelling strategies. Then write each Assessment Word under the unit number it fits. You will not write any words for Units 25 and 27.

Unit 25

It is important to spell words correctly that you use often in writing.

Unit 26

1.–3. The vowel sound in **new** can be spelled with the vowel digraph **ew**. The vowel sound in **cow** can be spelled with the vowel digraph **ow**.

Unit 27

Each color has a name. It is important to spell color words correctly.

Unit 28

4.–6. The /är/ sound you hear in **car** can be spelled **ar**.

Unit 29

7.–10. The **wh** digraph you hear at the beginning of **which** is spelled **wh**. The **ch** digraph you hear at the end of **which** is spelled **ch**.

bark

rich

gown

mew

jar

chat

whip

howl

card

wheels

CIRCUS

 **Review** Unit 25: Words Writers Use

want	many	off	saw	her

Write the spelling word to complete the sentence.

1. Last Friday we _____ the circus parade.
2. How _____ words did you write?
3. Emily went camping with _____ family.
4. Cross your name _____ if you are not going.
5. Do you _____ to buy some tickets?

 **Review** Unit 26: Vowel Digraphs ew, ow

new	grew	down	now	how

Write a spelling word for each of these clues.

6. It means the opposite of **old**. It rhymes with **few**.
7. This word is a form of the verb **grow**. It tells about something that happened in the past.
8. It rhymes with **cow**. It might come between **sooner** and **later**.
9. It is often used to start a question. Change one letter in **hop** to write this word.
10. It is the opposite of **up**. It rhymes with **clown**.

183

1.

2.

3.

4.

5.

6.

7.

8.

9.

10.

Review — Unit 27: Color Words

color	white	blue	green	red

Write spelling words to fit the clues.

1. This is the color of grass.
2. This is the color of the sky.
3. This is the color of a cloud.
4. This is the color of a valentine.
5. This word describes red or blue or green.

Review — Unit 28: r-Controlled a Spelled ar

car	farm	hard	park	part

Write a word that fits each shape.

6.    7. ▭▭▭   8. ▯▭▭▭

Write the spelling word that completes each sentence.

9. Which ____ of the book did you like?
10. Can you spot a good place to ____ our bikes?

chop	which	when	what	each

Write the spelling word by adding the missing letters.

1. ea __ __
2. __ __ op
3. __ __ en
4. __ __ at
5. whi __ __

 **Spelling Study Strategy**

Word Swap

Practicing spelling words can be fun if you make it into a game. Here's an idea you can try with a friend.

1. Swap spelling lists with a partner.

2. Ask your partner to read the first word on your list. Write the word on a piece of scrap paper.

3. Ask your partner to check your spelling. If you spelled the word correctly, your partner should say the next word on your list. If you did not spell the word correctly, ask your partner to spell the word out loud for you. Write the correct spelling.

4. Keep going until you have practiced five words. Then trade jobs. You will say the first word on your partner's list, and she or he will try to write the word correctly. Keep going until you and your partner have practiced all the words on your lists.

Unit 29

1.

2.

3.

4.

5.

185

WRITER'S

Grammar, Usage, and Mechanics

Verbs

A verb can tell what the subject of a sentence does or did.

The cow **jumped** over the moon.

A verb can also tell what the subject of a sentence is, was, or will be.

That cow **is** not real.

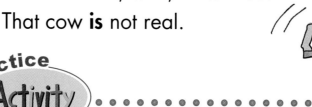

Practice Activity

A. Find the verb in each sentence. Write the verb.

1. Ramon fixed my notebook.
2. Someone answered the blue phone.
3. The dark living room was empty.
4. My new pet mouse sleeps a lot.

B. Complete each sentence with a verb from the box.

hard	grew	want	chop	down	saw

5. Last year I _____ four inches.
6. Yes, I _____ that red bird.
7. Ruth and I _____ more water.
8. We _____ wood every fall.

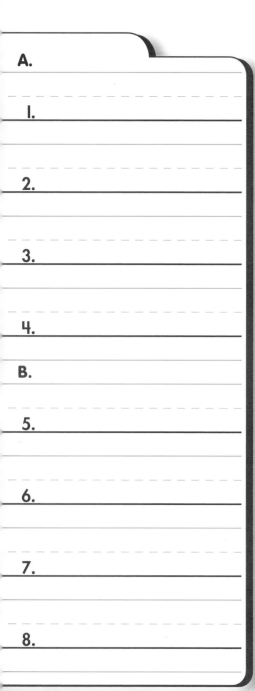

A.

1. _____

2. _____

3. _____

4. _____

B.

5. _____

6. _____

7. _____

8. _____

WORKSHOP

Box It In!

Good writers always proofread their writing for spelling mistakes. Here's a strategy that you should try.

Put your left pointer finger in front of a word. Put your right pointer finger after the word. Box in the word and check its spelling. Now look at another word the same way. Check each word that you wrote.

This way you will look hard at each word. You will notice mistakes. Try it!

Electronic Spelling

Search Engines

Search engines can help you find information. You type in a word or phrase. Then the search engine looks for that word or phrase. Search engines are not very smart, though. They cannot tell if you misspelled a word in your search. They will only look for the words you typed.

To make sure you find what you are looking for, type in several forms of common words. For instance, type **ant** and **ants**. Just be sure you spell both forms correctly.

One word in each pair is wrong. Write it correctly.

1. owl, wols   **2.** tree, tres   **3.** box, boxs

4. bird, brids   **5.** dich, dishes   **6.** clown, clownes

Electronic Spelling

1. _____

2. _____

3. _____

4. _____

5. _____

6. _____

oor

1. _____

ore

2. _____

3. _____

or

4. _____

5. _____

6. _____

7. _____

8. _____

9. _____

10. _____

Spelling and Thinking

READ THE SPELLING WORDS

1. for — What did you eat **for** lunch?
2. more — There are no **more** apples left.
3. corn — The **corn** grows in that field.
4. or — Jen **or** I will meet you there.
5. door — Shut the **door** when you leave.
6. fork — You need a **fork** to eat that.
7. horse — Tom will ride the small **horse**.
8. torn — Will you sew the **torn** pocket?
9. store — We buy bread at the **store**.
10. born — The baby was **born** yesterday.

SORT THE SPELLING WORDS

1. Write the word that spells the /ôr/ sound **oor**.
2.–3. Write the words that spell the /ôr/ sound **ore**.
4.–10. Write the words that spell the /ôr/ sound **or**.

REMEMBER THE SPELLING STRATEGY

Remember that the /ôr/ sound is spelled **or** in **for**, **ore** in **more**, and **oor** in **door**.

Spelling ᵃⁿᵈ Phonics

Word Structure

Take one letter away from each word to make a spelling word. Write each spelling word.

  1. four   **2.** ore   **3.** hoarse

Word Analysis

Write the spelling word that fits each clue.

  4. It rhymes with **horn** and begins like **coat**.

  5. It contains the words **do** and **or**.

  6. It begins with a consonant cluster.

  7. It has four letters and contains the spelling word with three letters.

Guide words help you find words in a dictionary. Write the spelling words that would be found between these sets of guide words.

  8. took • wave

  9. meet • nail

  10. bedroom • bring

Word Structure

  1. _____

  2. _____

  3. _____

Word Analysis

  4. _____

  5. _____

  6. _____

  7. _____

Using the Dictionary

  8. _____

  9. _____

  10. _____

for	more	corn	or	door
fork	horse	torn	store	born

Complete the Groups

1. _____

2. _____

3. _____

4. _____

5. _____

Complete the Paragraph

6. _____

7. _____

8. _____

9. _____

10. _____

Complete the Groups Write the spelling word that belongs in each group.

1. spoon, knife, _____

2. peas, carrots, _____

3. donkey, zebra, _____

4. stairs, window, roof, _____

5. ripped, split, _____

Complete the Paragraph
Write spelling words to complete the paragraph.

My new cousin was __6.__ on March 13. Everyone was so happy to get the news. I wanted to get a special present __7.__ her. The question was what to get. I went to the __8.__ with my mom. There we saw many things. In the end, I did not know whether to get her a rattle __9.__ a bib. Mom laughed and said, "Do not worry. You will get her __10.__ presents later!"

Spelling and Writing

Proofread an Ad

Four words are not spelled correctly in this ad.
Write the words correctly.

Looking foar toys?
SHOP AT STAR'S!

Star's Toy Shop is having a sale on
everything! Visit our stoor next Thursday,
Friday, or Saturday. The first 20 people at
the dore win a prize! Shop at Star's, or
pay moar somewhere else!

Write an Ad

Persuasive Writing

Write an ad for a sale at your favorite store. Be
sure to tell
- when and where the sale will be.
- what will be on sale.
- why people should come.

Use as many spelling words as you can.

Writing Process

Prewriting
⇩
Drafting
⇩
Revising
⇩
Proofread Your Writing During ➤ **Editing**
⇩
Publishing

Proofread your writing for spelling errors as part
of the editing stage in the writing process. Be sure
to check each word carefully. Use a dictionary to
check spelling if you are not sure.

Vocabulary

Strategy Words

Review Words

1. _____

2. _____

3. _____

Preview Words

4. _____

5. _____

6. _____

Review Words: r-Controlled o Spelled or, ore

Write the word from the box that fits each clue.

hope	note	rope

1. You will find **o** and **r** in this word, but it has **long o** spelled **vowel-consonant-e**.

2. This word begins like **normal,** but it has the **long o** sound.

3. This word begins and ends like **horse,** but it has a different vowel sound.

Preview Words: r-Controlled o Spelled or, ore

Write the word from the box that fits each clue.

explore	morning	storm

4. It means "to look."

5. It is the opposite of **evening**.

6. It can bring wind, rain, or snow.

Connections

Content Words

Social Studies: Clothing

Write words from the box to complete the paragraph.

cord	loom	yarn	weave

Did you know that most cloth is made by machine? Workers use machines to spin wool into thread, or __1.__ . They put the yarn on a machine called a __2.__ . Then they __3.__ the yarn into cloth. They use different colors of yarn to make designs in the cloth. When they are done, they sometimes roll up the cloth and tie it with a __4.__ .

Apply the Spelling Strategy

Circle the letters that spell the /ôr/ sound in one of the content words you wrote.

Social Studies: Clothing

1. _____

2. _____

3. _____

4. _____

four-letter word, begins with sh

1. _____

five-letter words, begin with sh

2. _____

3. _____

4. _____

5. _____

four-letter words, end with sh

6. _____

7. _____

8. _____

9. _____

10. _____

Spelling and Thinking

READ THE SPELLING WORDS

1. shine — The sun might **shine** later.
2. rush — People **rush** to catch the bus.
3. shoe — That **shoe** fits my foot.
4. cash — Ten dollars is a lot of **cash**!
5. short — One block is a **short** distance.
6. dash — They **dash** to the finish line.
7. bush — This **bush** has small leaves.
8. shore — We find shells at the **shore**.
9. wash — Please **wash** with soap.
10. shout — I must **shout** so Liz can hear.

SORT THE SPELLING WORDS

1. Write the four-letter spelling word that begins with **sh**.
2.–5. Write the five-letter spelling words that begin with **sh**.
6.–10. Write the four-letter spelling words that end with **sh**.

REMEMBER THE SPELLING STRATEGY

Remember that the /**sh**/ sound you hear in **shoe** and **bush** can be spelled **sh**.

Spelling and Phonics

Word Analysis

Write the spelling word that fits each clue.

1. This word rhymes with **or**.
2. This word contains the smaller word **out**.
3. This word ends like **mine**.
4. This word rhymes with **sort**. It has one more letter than **sort**.

Sound and Letter Patterns

Write spelling words by adding the missing letters.

5. wa __ __
6. ru __ __
7. b __ __ h
8. __ __ oe

USING THE Dictionary

Write the spelling words that fit these dictionary meanings.

9. **a.** money **b.** to exchange for money
10. **a.** a punctuation mark that looks like this:— **b.** a small amount

Spelling and Reading

shine	rush	shoe	cash	short
dash	bush	shore	wash	shout

Complete the Groups Write the spelling word that belongs in each group.

1. sneaker, sandal, _____
2. race, broad jump, high jump, _____
3. hurry, speed, _____
4. small, low, _____

Name the Category Write the spelling word that names each group of words.

5. dollars, coins, money
6. Hey! Stop! Hurray!

Complete the Sentences Write the spelling word that completes each sentence.

7. You cannot see the sun _____ in the sky on a cloudy day.
8. I saw a seal resting in the sun on the sandy _____.
9. I will _____ this dirty cup.
10. The leaves on that _____ turn bright red in the fall.

Complete the Groups

1.
2.
3.
4.

Name the Category

5.
6.

Complete the Sentences

7.
8.
9.
10.

196

Spelling and Writing

Proofread a Paragraph

Four words are not spelled correctly in this paragraph. Write the words correctly.

Our car was dirty. We were in a big russ to get it clean. My dad and I took it to the car wassh. In a very short time, it came out so clean! It even seemed to sine! My dad was so pleased with it. The car looked better than it had in a long time. I thought he would showt for joy!

Proofreading Marks

≡ Make a capital.

/ Make a small letter.

∧ Add something.

℮ Take out something.

⊙ Add a period.

⌗ New paragraph

SP Spelling error

Write a Paragraph

Narrative Writing

Tell about any event in your life. It does not have to be something big or important. Tell

- who was there.
- what happened.
- where it took place.

Use as many spelling words as you can.

Writing Process

Prewriting

⇩

Drafting

⇩

Revising

⇩

Proofread Your Writing During ▶ **Editing**

⇩

Publishing

Proofread your writing for spelling errors as part of the editing stage in the writing process. Be sure to check each word carefully. Use a dictionary to check spelling if you are not sure.

Vocabulary

Strategy Words

Review Words

_____
1. _____

_____
2. _____

_____
3. _____

Preview Words

_____
4. _____

_____
5. _____

_____
6. _____

Review Words: sh

Write the word from the box that fits each clue.

hush	she	shop

1. This word can mean the same as "store."
2. This word can mean the same as "quiet."
3. This word can be used in place of a girl's name.

Preview Words: sh

Write the word from the box that fits each clue.

bushel	fresh	shaggy

4. This word has **sh** in the middle.
5. This word has two syllables and the **long e** sound.
6. This word has one syllable.

Connections

Content Words

Language Arts: Exact Meanings

Write the word from the box that could best take the place of the underlined word or words.

harm	litter	junk	trash

1. Too much water will <u>hurt</u> the flowers.
2. Will you put the banana peel in the <u>garbage</u> can?
3. The attic was filled with boxes and old <u>useless things</u>.
4. Our class picked up <u>bits of paper and garbage</u> to make the playground safe and beautiful.

Apply the Spelling Strategy

Circle the content word you wrote that has the /**sh**/ sound.

Show you care, RECYCLE Your Share

Language Arts: Exact Meanings

1.
2.
3.
4.

Spelling and Thinking

begin with th

1. _____

2. _____

3. _____

4. _____

5. _____

6. _____

end with th

7. _____

8. _____

9. _____

10. _____

READ THE SPELLING WORDS

1.	they	Are **they** the boys you saw?
2.	teeth	I brush my **teeth** often.
3.	those	We like **those** pants in the window.
4.	than	Steve is taller **than** Mindy.
5.	tooth	My front **tooth** is loose.
6.	these	I made **these** cards myself.
7.	moth	The **moth** flies into the light.
8.	them	I had toys, but I lost **them**.
9.	both	I like **both** Ann and Brad.
10.	thank	Did you **thank** Jed for helping us?

SORT THE SPELLING WORDS

1.–6. Write the spelling words that begin with **th**.

7.–10. Write the spelling words that end with **th**.

REMEMBER THE SPELLING STRATEGY

Remember that the **th** digraph you hear at the beginning of **these** and at the end of **teeth** is spelled **th**.

Spelling ^{and} Phonics

Word Structure

1. Remove one letter from **booth** to make a spelling word.
2. Change one letter in **math** to make a spelling word.
3. Change two letters in **thing** to make a spelling word.

Sound and Letter Patterns

Write spelling words by adding the missing letters.

4. __ hose
5. __ __ an
6. too __ __
7. tee __ __

The words in a dictionary are in a-b-c order.

8.–10. Write these spelling words in a-b-c order. If the first three letters in words are the same, use the fourth letter to put them in a-b-c order.

these   they   them

Word Structure

1.

2.

3.

Sound and Letter Patterns

4.

5.

6.

7.

Using the Dictionary

8.

9.

10.

Complete the Paragraphs

1. _____
2. _____
3. _____
4. _____
5. _____
6. _____
7. _____
8. _____
9. _____
10. _____

they	teeth	those	than	tooth
these	moth	them	both	thank

Complete the Paragraphs Write the spelling words that complete the paragraphs.

When was the last time you lost a __1.__? Did you know that your first __2.__ are called primary teeth? You probably know that __3.__ are also called baby teeth.

There are ten primary teeth in __4.__ the upper and lower jaws. When __5.__ teeth fall out, there is room for the second set of teeth. There are more teeth in the second set __6.__ there are in the first set.

Your teeth are very important. You should take good care of __7.__. You should brush after meals, try not to eat too many sweets, floss once a day, and visit your dentist often. If you follow __8.__ rules, your teeth will be healthy. Someday you will __9.__ your parents for saying, "Go brush your teeth!"

Here is a riddle about teeth. What does a __10.__ need to have a smile and teeth? It needs the letter **u**!

Spelling and Writing

Proofread a Thank-You Note

Four words are not spelled correctly in this thank-you note. Write the words correctly.

Dear Grandpa,

Thank you for thos toys you sent. I play that board game more thin any other game. I also like the spaceship and launch pad. I think thay are boath cool!

Love,

Jimmy

Proofreading Marks

≡   Make a capital.

／   Make a small letter.

∧   Add something.

℘   Take out something.

⊙   Add a period.

⌗   New paragraph

SP   Spelling error

Write a Thank-You Note

Expository Writing

Write a thank-you note to someone who has done something nice for you. Be sure to

- begin with **Dear**.
- use commas after your greeting and your closing.
- tell what you are thankful for.

Use as many spelling words as you can.

Writing Process

Prewriting

⇩

Drafting

⇩

Revising

⇩

Proofread Your Writing During ➤ Editing

⇩

Publishing

Proofread your writing for spelling errors as part of the editing stage in the writing process. Be sure to check each word carefully. Use a dictionary to check spelling if you are not sure.

Vocabulary

Strategy Words

Review Words

1. _____

2. _____

3. _____

Preview Words

4. _____

5. _____

6. _____

Review Words: th

Write a word from the box to complete each sentence.

the	then	with

1. You can look up words in _____ dictionary.

2. We ate lunch, and _____ we played baseball.

3. I am going to the play _____ my mom.

Preview Words: th

Write the word from the box that completes each analogy.

father	smooth	thumb

4. **Hard** is to **soft** as **rough** is to _____.

5. **Girl** is to **boy** as **mother** is to _____.

6. **Foot** is to **big toe** as **hand** is to _____.

Connections

Content Words

Write the word from the box that fits each clue.

first	third	second	fourth

1. This word comes after **second** and before **fourth**.
2. This word names the place of the person in the front of a line.
3. This word is the closest to **first**.
4. This place in line comes before fifth place.

Apply the Spelling Strategy

Circle the letters that spell the **th** digraph in two of the content words you wrote.

Math: Ordinal Numbers

1. _____

2. _____

3. _____

4. _____

205

r-controlled vowel

1. _____
2. _____
3. _____
4. _____

long vowel sound

5. _____
6. _____
7. _____
8. _____

ou

9. _____
10. _____

Spelling and Thinking

READ THE SPELLING WORDS

1. deer — The **deer** lives in the woods.
2. here — Please be **here** by noon.
3. meet — I will **meet** you at the store.
4. tale — She told a funny **tale**.
5. hour — We will be ready in an **hour**.
6. tail — The dog wagged its **tail**.
7. hear — Did you **hear** a bell ring?
8. dear — He is a very **dear** friend.
9. our — We will show you **our** pictures.
10. meat — Dad likes mustard on his **meat**.

SORT THE SPELLING WORDS

1.–4. Write the homophone pairs that have an **r**-controlled vowel.

5.–8. Write the homophone pairs that have a long vowel sound.

9.–10. Write the homophone pair spelled with **ou**.

REMEMBER THE SPELLING STRATEGY

Remember that **homophones** are words that sound the same but have different spellings and meanings. **Hear** and **here** are homophones.

Spelling ^{and} Phonics

Word Analysis

1. Write the word that has three letters and begins with two vowels.
2. Write the word that spells the **long a** sound **ai**.
3. Write the word that begins like **dog** and ends with **ear**.
4. Write the word made by changing one letter in **beet**.

Replace the Words

Write the spelling word that takes the place of each incorrect homophone.

5. The <u>dear</u> ran quickly across the road.
6. Mom put a piece of <u>meet</u> on the grill.
7. "Cinderella" is a fairy <u>tail</u>.

The words in a dictionary are in a-b-c order.

8.–10. Write these spelling words in a-b-c order.

here   hear   hour

◆ ◆ ◆

Dictionary Check Be sure to check the a-b-c order of the words in your **Spelling Dictionary**.

Word Analysis

1. _____

2. _____

3. _____

4. _____

Replace the Words

5. _____

6. _____

7. _____

Using the Dictionary

8. _____

9. _____

10. _____

Spelling and Reading

deer	here	meet	tale	hour
tail	hear	dear	our	meat

Complete the Groups Write the spelling word that fits in each group.

1. ears, paws, nose, _____
2. see, taste, touch, smell, _____
3. moose, elk, _____

Solve the Analogies Write the spelling word that completes each analogy.

4. **Notes** are to **song** as **words** are to _____.
5. **Good-bye** is to **leave** as **hello** is to _____.
6. **This** is to **that** as _____ is to **there**.

Choose the Word Write the word in parentheses that correctly completes each sentence.

7. We will have (meet, meat), potatoes, and vegetables for dinner.
8. Shana is a (deer, dear) friend of mine.
9. Bart and I waited an (hour, our) for the school bus today.
10. Next week the mayor of our town will visit (hour, our) class.

208

Spelling and Writing

Proofread a Diary Entry

Four words are not spelled correctly in this diary entry. Write the words correctly.

Proofreading Marks

≡ Make a capital.

/ Make a small letter.

∧ Add something.

℘ Take out something.

⊙ Add a period.

⌗ New paragraph

SP Spelling error

Dear Diary,   June 13

We are hear! It's the top of Bald Mountain. Mom and I had a great hike. We traveled along a cold, clear stream for the first our. Then we saw a dear! It ran right across our path. It had soft brown fur and a big white tale.

Write a Diary Entry

Descriptive Writing

Write a diary entry. Describe something you have seen or done. Be sure to include

- details about what you saw, heard, touched, smelled, or felt.
- what made it special.

Use as many spelling words as you can.

Writing Process

Prewriting
⇩
Drafting
⇩
Revising
⇩
Editing
⇩
Publishing

Proofread Your Writing During Editing

Proofread your writing for spelling errors as part of the editing stage in the writing process. Be sure to check each word carefully. Use a dictionary to check spelling if you are not sure.

Vocabulary

Strategy Words

Review Words

1. _____
_____
2. _____
_____
3. _____

Preview Words

4. _____
_____
5. _____
_____
6. _____

Review Words: Homophones

Write the word from the box that completes each sentence.

be	son	sun

1. Will you _____ the bee in our play?
2. I wear a hat to shade my eyes from the _____.
3. Mrs. Tajima came with her oldest _____.

Preview Words: Homophones

Write the word from the box that fits each clue.

grate	great	hare

4. It sounds like **hair,** but it names an animal like a rabbit.
5. It means the opposite of "very small."
6. It means "to shred."

Connections

Content Words

Science: Human Body

Write the word from the box that matches each meaning.

heel	sole	shin	toe

1. part of the leg below the knee and above the ankle
2. the bottom of the foot or the bottom of a shoe
3. one of the five parts at the front end of a foot
4. part of the back end of the foot, below the ankle

Science: Human Body

1. _____
2. _____
3. _____
4. _____

Apply the Spelling Strategy

Circle the content words you wrote that are homophones for these words: **heal, soul,** and **tow**.

Spelling and Thinking

two-letter words

1. _____

2. _____

3. _____

three-letter words

4. _____

5. _____

6. _____

7. _____

two four-letter words

8. _____

9. _____

10. _____

READ THE SPELLING WORDS

1.	inside	The dog is **inside** the fence.
2.	myself	I made **myself** a sandwich.
3.	bedroom	I sleep in this **bedroom**.
4.	football	Who threw that **football**?
5.	birthday	I will be ten on my **birthday**.
6.	downtown	We shop in the **downtown** area.
7.	baseball	I like the game of **baseball**.
8.	cannot	Len can dive, but I **cannot**.
9.	outside	The dog can go **outside** now.
10.	into	I pour water **into** my glass.

SORT THE SPELLING WORDS

1.–3. Write the compound words that contain two-letter words.

4.–7. Write the compound words that contain three-letter words.

8.–10. Write the compound words that contain two four-letter words.

REMEMBER THE SPELLING STRATEGY

Remember that a **compound word** is formed from two or more words to make a new word:
can + not = cannot.

Spelling ^and Phonics

Word Analysis

Two words in each sentence can make a compound spelling word. Write the compound word.

1. You can go in if you want to.

2. Mom drove down the road to the end of town.

3. There is space for only one bed in this room.

4. Sometimes I get a pain in my side from running.

5. A small animal ran out from the side of the road.

6. Ling threw the ball to second base.

Word Structure

Replace the underlined syllable to write a spelling word.

7. <u>her</u>self   8. <u>week</u>day

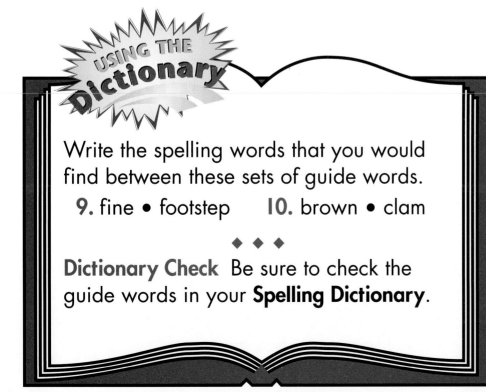

USING THE Dictionary

Write the spelling words that you would find between these sets of guide words.

9. fine • footstep   10. brown • clam

◆ ◆ ◆

Dictionary Check Be sure to check the guide words in your **Spelling Dictionary**.

Word Analysis

1. _____

2. _____

3. _____

4. _____

5. _____

6. _____

Word Structure

7. _____

8. _____

Using the Dictionary

9. _____

10. _____

Spelling and Reading

inside   myself   into   baseball
birthday   downtown   bedroom   football
outside   cannot

Complete the Groups Write the spelling word that belongs in each group.

1. indoors, in the house, _____
2. yourself, themselves, _____
3. does not, did not, _____

Complete the Sentences Write the spelling word that completes each sentence.

4. It is a beautiful day, so we should go _____ to play!
5. He kicked the _____ forty yards.
6. Many big city buildings are being built _____.
7. Sandy hit a home run at the _____ game.
8. The girl dove _____ the deep end of the pool.

Replace the Words Write the spelling word that could take the place of the underlined words in each sentence.

9. I have pictures of my favorite basketball players on the walls of my <u>room with a bed</u>.
10. This year my parents gave me a new winter coat on my <u>day of birth</u>.

Complete the Groups
1.
2.
3.

Complete the Sentences
4.
5.
6.
7.
8.

Replace the Words
9.
10.

214

Spelling and Writing

Proofread a Letter

Four words are not spelled correctly in this letter. Write the words correctly.

Dear Jake,

I hope you are coming to my birtday party. We will play baseball and football outside. Then we will go insied to eat cake. We will have a lot of fun. If you canot come, you will miss a great party. I will miss you, too.

Your friend,

Billy

Proofreading Marks

≡ Make a capital.

/ Make a small letter.

∧ Add something.

℮ Take out something.

⊙ Add a period.

⌗ New paragraph

SP Spelling error

Write a Letter _____ Persuasive Writing

Write a short letter. Persuade a friend to do something fun. Be sure to

- tell what you will do.
- give reasons to persuade your friend to join you.

Use as many spelling words as you can.

Writing Process

Prewriting

⇩

Drafting

⇩

Revising

⇩

Proofread Your Writing During Editing

⇩

Publishing

Proofread your writing for spelling errors as part of the editing stage in the writing process. Be sure to check each word carefully. Use a dictionary to check spelling if you are not sure.

Vocabulary

Strategy Words

Review Words

1. _____

2. _____

3. _____

Preview Words

4. _____

5. _____

6. _____

Review Words: Compound Words

Write a word from the box to complete each set of directions.

lace	neck	tub

1. bath + _____ = bathtub
2. neck + _____ = necklace
3. _____ + lace = necklace

Preview Words: Compound Words

Write the word from the box that fits each clue.

beeswax	foghorn	rowboat

4. This word begins like **fat** and ends like **corn**.

5. Part of this word rhymes with **low**.

6. Part of this word rhymes with **ax**.

Connections

Content Words

Health: Hygiene

Write the word from the box that fits each clue.

fingernail	scrub	skin	toenail

1. This word rhymes with **tub**. It goes with **wash** and **shine**.
2. This word names part of your hand.
3. This word names part of your foot.
4. This word rhymes with **fin**. It names something that covers your whole body.

Apply the Spelling Strategy

Circle the two content words you wrote that are compound words.

Health: Hygiene

1. _____
2. _____
3. _____
4. _____

1. _____

2. _____

3. _____

Unit 32

4. _____

5. _____

Unit 33

6. _____

7. _____

Unit 34

8. _____

9. _____

Unit 35

10. _____

Assessment and Review

Assessment Units 31–35

Each Assessment Word in the box fits one of the spelling strategies you have studied over the past five weeks. Read the spelling strategies. Then write each Assessment Word under the unit number it fits.

Unit 31_____
1.–3. The /ôr/ sound is spelled **or** in **for**, **ore** in **more,** and **oor** in **door**.

Unit 32_____
4.–5. The /sh/ sound you hear in **shoe** and **bush** can be spelled **sh**.

Unit 33_____
6.–7. The **th** digraph you hear at the beginning of **these** and at the end of **teeth** is spelled **th**.

Unit 34_____
8.–9. Homophones are words that sound the same but have different spellings and meanings. **Hear** and **here** are homophones.

Unit 35_____
10. A **compound word** is formed from two or more words to make a new word: **can + not = cannot**.

sail
cloth
horn
chore
crush
doorstep
thing
pancake
shack
sale

 **Review** Unit 31: r-Controlled o Spelled or, ore

born	horse	store	door	for

Follow the directions to write spelling words.

1. nor – n + f = _____
2. deer – ee + oo = _____
3. horn – n + se = _____
4. barn – a + o = _____
5. core – c + st = _____

 **Review** Unit 32: sh

shoe	wash	short	bush	shore

Write a spelling word that rhymes with the underlined word and fits the sentence.

6. We stood on the <u>core</u> to watch the waves.

7. This pencil is too <u>sport</u>.

8. The bird sat on the <u>push</u>.

Write the spelling word that fits each shape.

9.

10.

1. _____

2. _____

3. _____

4. _____

5. _____

6. _____

7. _____

8. _____

9. _____

10. _____

Review Unit 33: th

than	them	they	both	these

Write the spelling word that completes each sentence.

1. This tree is taller _____ my house.

2. Sarah and her friends are coming, and _____ will be here soon.

3. Be sure to bring _____ a pencil and a ruler to class.

4. You can take those books. I want to keep _____ to read myself.

5. I know Jeff and Jorge are here. I saw _____ in the hall.

Review Unit 34: Homophones

hear	our	here	hour	tail

Write the word that fits with the others.

6. second, minute, _____

7. _____, there, everywhere

8. head, paws, _____

9. my, your, _____

10. see, taste, _____

Unit 35: Compound Words

| into | birthday | outside | cannot | inside |

Match one word from each column to make a spelling word. Write the word.

1. in   not
2. out   side
3. in   day
4. can   to
5. birth   side

 **Spelling Study Strategy**

Sorting by Spelling Patterns

Here is a good way to practice your spelling words. Place the words into groups by their spelling patterns.

1. Make three columns on a large piece of paper or on the chalkboard.

2. Write one spelling pattern at the top of each column:
   (1) **or, ore, oor**
   (2) **sh**
   (3) **th**

3. Have a partner say a spelling word from Unit 31, 32, or 33.

4. Write the spelling word in the column that shows the spelling pattern.

Unit 35

1. _____
2. _____
3. _____
4. _____
5. _____

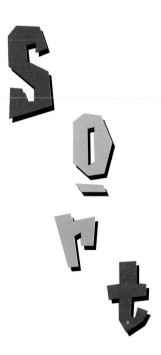

Grammar, Usage, and Mechanics

Adjectives

An adjective describes, or tells about, a noun. It can tell what kind, how much, or how many.

I like your **red** sweater.

Many trees have flowers.

Molly made a **small** salad.

Practice Activity

A. Write the adjective in each sentence.

   1. Chris has a new pair of shoes.

   2. A black dog trotted into the yard.

   3. I gave flowers to my dear friend.

   4. The menu has several sandwiches.

B. Complete each sentence with an adjective from the box.

white	short	both	slow

   5. You may have _____ apples.

   6. Jim wore a _____ shirt and tan pants.

   7. The rope was too _____ to make a swing.

   8. This is a very _____ bus ride!

A.

1.

2.

3.

4.

B.

5.

6.

7.

8.

WORKSHOP

Circle and Check

Good writers always proofread their writing for spelling mistakes. Here's a strategy that you should try.

Look at the first word. Ask yourself if it is spelled right. If you are sure that it is, go on. Read the next word. If you are not sure about the spelling, though, circle the word. Then keep reading.

Check all the circled words when you have finished proofreading. Look them all up at one time in a dictionary. Try it!

Electronic Spelling

Help Programs

A **help program** shows you how to do things on a computer. To use it, you type in words, such as **opening a file**. Then the help program tells you how to open a file.

Make sure you spell words with **-ing** endings correctly. If you misspell **opening,** the program can't help you learn how to open a file.

Which of these words are misspelled? Write them correctly. Write **OK** if a word is correct.

1. cuting	2. copying	3. moveing
4. searching	5. pasteing	6. saveing

Electronic Spelling

1. _____

2. _____

3. _____

4. _____

5. _____

6. _____

223

| basket | napkins | salad | wagon |

A.

1.

2.

3.

4.

B.

1.

2.

3.

4.

A. Write the challenge word that goes with each group.

1. bus, car, bike
2. purse, bag, pocket
3. plates, cups, forks
4. soup, bread, fruit

B. Write a challenge word to complete each sentence.

1. Ann set the basket in the _____.
2. We wipe our hands with _____.
3. Fred ate a _____ for lunch.
4. The farmer carried eggs in a _____.

C. Terry and Jan go on a picnic. Write about what they do. Use the challenge words in your story.

Challenge Activities

| melon | celery | lettuce | vegetable |

A. Write a challenge word for each clue.

1. I am a long, thin, and crunchy vegetable.
2. My wide leaves are used in salads.
3. I am round, sweet, and juicy.
4. I grow in the garden. Lettuce, peas, and corn belong to my family.

B. Write a challenge word to answer each question.

1. Which word has the little word **let** in it?
2. Which word has both **get** and **able** in it?
3. Which word has both **me** and **on** in it?
4. Which word starts like **cent** and ends like **very**?

C. Mr. Hippity-Hop is fixing lunch. Write about what he will have for lunch. Use the challenge words.

A.

1.

2.

3.

4.

B.

1.

2.

3.

4.

Challenge Activities

crisp   twist   nibble   wiggle

A. Write a challenge word to finish each sentence.

1. This lettuce is fresh and _____.
2. Can you _____ the lid off this jar?
3. Albert can _____ his ears.
4. I'd like a _____ of that cheese.
5. We came to a _____ in the road.
6. These goldfish _____ on their food.
7. Worms _____ in the dirt.
8. We had apple _____ for dessert.

B. Reread each sentence in Part A. Next to the words you wrote, write **N** if the challenge word is a naming word. Write **A** if the challenge word tells about an action. Write **D** if the challenge word describes something. Some of the challenge words can be used in more than one way.

C. Write a story about the picture. Use the challenge words.

A./B.

1. _____
2. _____
3. _____
4. _____
5. _____
6. _____
7. _____
8. _____

Challenge Activities

| smock | model | hobby | bonnet |

A. Write a challenge word for each definition.

1. a kind of hat

2. a loose covering to protect clothing

3. a small copy of something

4. something you do for fun

B. Complete this make-believe story with the challenge words.

Harriet Hippo likes to sew. That is her __1.__. She also likes to __2.__ her clothes for her friends. Today she has a new __3.__ on her head. It matches the __4.__ she is wearing.

C. Read the following definitions of the word **model**. Then write a sentence for each definition. Write three sentences in all.

model 1. A small copy of something. 2. A person who wears clothes to show to others. 3. To wear clothes to show to others.

A.
1.
2.
3.
4.
B.
1.
2.
3.
4.

227

Challenge Activities

gruff   stump   tumble   puddle

A.
1.
2.
3.
4.
B.
1.
2.
3.
4.

A. Add and subtract letters to make challenge words.

1. stuff – st + gr = _____
2. stamp – a + u = _____
3. paddle – a + u = _____
4. tummy – my + ble = _____

B. Write a challenge word to complete each rhyme.

1. I'm all in a muddle
   Since I stepped in that _____.
2. The giant was tough.
   When he spoke, he was _____.
3. Be careful not to bump
   Into that old tree _____.
4. If you stumble,
   You might take a _____.

C. Use the challenge words to write about this rhyme. Answer the question about George.

George the giant is gruff today. What might have happened to make him this way?

Challenge Activities

mall	stall	squall	stalk

A. Write a challenge word to finish each sentence.

1. We shop in the _____.

2. Please don't _____.

3. The horse sleeps in a _____.

4. The corn grows on a _____.

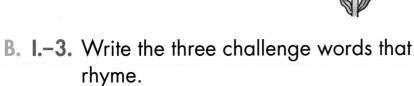

B. **1.–3.** Write the three challenge words that rhyme.

   4. Write the challenge word that rhymes with **walk**.

C. One meaning of the word **squall** is "a sudden storm." Pretend you were outside. Suddenly a squall began. What was it like? What did you do? Write about what happened.

A.

1. _____

2. _____

3. _____

4. _____

B.

1. _____

2. _____

3. _____

4. _____

Challenge Activities

frisky   grumpy   fluffy   glossy

A. Write the challenge words that rhyme with the words below.

1. bumpy, jumpy
2. huffy, puffy
3. mossy, bossy
4. risky

B. 1.–4. Write the challenge words in a-b-c order. If the first letter in two words is the same, look at the second letter.

C. Pretend you are at a zoo. Use the challenge words to tell about the animals you see.

A.

_1._

_2._

_3._

_4._

B.

_1._

_2._

_3._

_4._

Challenge Activities

swing   blink   cranky   finger

A. Write a challenge word to finish each sentence.

  1. The baby was tired and _____.
  2. When the sun is bright, I _____ my eyes.
  3. Carol has a pretty ring on her _____.
  4. Dad pushed me on the _____.

B. Write the challenge word that completes each group.

  1. mad, grumpy, _____
  2. twinkle, wink, _____
  3. wrist, hand, _____
  4. slide, seesaw, _____

C. Have you ever felt cranky? What made you cranky? How does it feel to be cranky? What did you do to cheer yourself up? Write about it.

A.

1.

2.

3.

4.

B.

1.

2.

3.

4.

Challenge Activities

glove   gone   shiver   shovel

A. Write a challenge word to finish the second sentence in each pair.

1. After you do something, it has been done. After you go away, you have _____.
2. You put a sock on your foot. You put a _____ on your hand.
3. You sweep with a broom. You dig with a _____.
4. When it's hot, you sweat. When it's cold, you _____.

B. Say each challenge word to yourself. Answer the questions.

1.–2. Which challenge words have one syllable?

3.–4. Which challenge words have two syllables?

C. What is it like on a cold, snowy day? What might you do on such a day? Use the challenge words to write about it.

A.

1.

2.

3.

4.

B.

1.

2.

3.

4.

Challenge Activities

chute	crate	twine	zone

A. Write challenge words to complete the picture.

This is a ___1.___ of apples. It is tied with ___2.___ .

Let it down the ___3.___ .

NO PARKING ___4.___

B. Write a challenge word for each definition.

1. a wooden box
2. a special area
3. a slide or tube used to send things down
4. a strong string

C. What happens in a school zone? What do cars and people do when they see a school zone sign? Write some sentences to tell about it.

A. _____

1. _____

2. _____

3. _____

4. _____

B. _____

1. _____

2. _____

3. _____

4. _____

Challenge Activities

| stain | daisy | spray | plate |

A. 1.–4. Write each challenge word. Then circle the letters in each word that spell the **long a** sound.

A.

1.

2.

3.

4.

B. Look at the picture and the numbers. Write the challenge word for each number.

B.

1.

2.

3.

4.

C. Look at the picture in Part B. Write a story about what is happening. Use the challenge words.

Challenge Activities

| easel | teach | seek | sneeze |

A. Write a challenge word to finish each sentence.

1. Mary paints at an _____.

2. Dust makes Ted _____.

3. Sam and Mia play hide-and-_____.

4. Mr. Lin will _____ us to add.

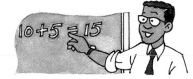

B. Write the challenge word that rhymes with each word.

1. peek   2. beach   3. breeze   4. weasel

C. There are lots of different games. Hide-and-seek is one of them. What are some games you like to play? List them. Then tell why you like to play them.

A. _____

1. _____

2. _____

3. _____

4. _____

B. _____

1. _____

2. _____

3. _____

4. _____

235

Challenge Activities

mime   spice   pry   nylon

A. Write the challenge word that goes with each picture.

1.   2.   3.   4.

B. Write a challenge word to finish each sentence.

1. This tent is made of _____.
2. The _____ acted out a story.
3. Pepper is a kind of _____.
4. The lid is stuck, so we will _____ it off.

C. The word **mime** means "to act out a story without talking." Think of a story you can act out without talking. Your story can be very short. Write some things you might "tell." Put them in order. Write what you might do first, next, and last. Perhaps you can act out your story for your classmates. They can try to figure out what your story is about.

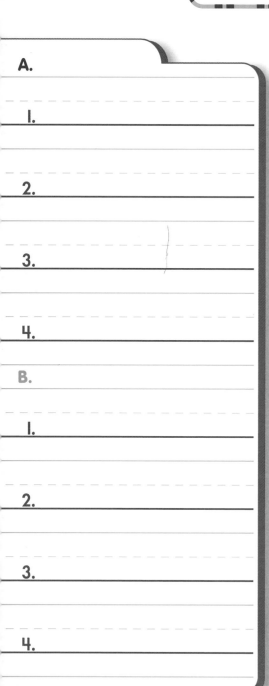

A.
1. _____
2. _____
3. _____
4. _____
B.
1. _____
2. _____
3. _____
4. _____

Challenge Activities

| coach | roast | golden | follow |

A. Write challenge words to complete the story.

    Long ago there lived a king and queen. They both wore __1.__ crowns. One day they went on a trip. They rode in a big __2.__ pulled by horses. At night they came to an inn. "Let's eat and sleep here," they said. The king and queen ate a meal of tasty __3.__ beef. After dinner, the innkeeper said, "Please __4.__ me. I will show you to your room."

B. Change two letters in each word to make a challenge word. Write the challenge words.

    1. bellow   **2.** boost   **3.** coast   **4.** holder

C. What things are golden? Make a list of them. Then write a story about one of the things on your list.

A.

1.

2.

3.

4.

B.

1.

2.

3.

4.

237

Challenge Activities

| cast | pike | dock | tackle |

A. Write challenge words to complete the story.

Nan and her dad had their fishing poles and __1.__ box. They stood on a __2.__ over the lake. Nan __3.__ her line in the water. She caught a big fish.

"That fish is a __4.__," her dad said.

B. Each challenge word in the list has more than one meaning. Write a challenge word for each definition.

1. all of the people who act in a movie or play
2. to grab hold of and throw to the ground
3. to steer a boat to a resting place
4. a big road

C. Write a sentence about each picture. Use the word **cast** in each sentence.

A.

1.

2.

3.

4.

B.

1.

2.

3.

4.

Challenge Activities

| braid | grease | pleat | sleeve |

A. Write a challenge word to go with each clue.

  1. You can use this on a bike chain.

  2. A girl might fix her hair this way.

  3. You put your arm in this.

  4. This can be part of a skirt.

B. A smaller word is hidden in each challenge word. Read the words below. Write the challenge words that have these hidden words in them.

  1. eve   **2.** ease

  3. eat   **4.** raid

C. Describe the person you see in the picture. Who do you think she is? What does she look like? What is she going to do? Use as many challenge words as you can.

A. _____

1. _____

2. _____

3. _____

4. _____

B. _____

1. _____

2. _____

3. _____

4. _____

Challenge Activities

eleven   twelve   thirteen   fourteen

A.

I.

2.

3.

4.

B.

I.

2.

3.

4.

A. Write a challenge word to solve each problem.

I. $15 - 3 = $ _____

2. $20 - 9 = $ _____

3. $7 + 7 = $ _____

4. $8 + 5 = $ _____

B. Say each challenge word to yourself. Then write challenge words to answer the questions.

   I. Which word has one syllable?

   2.–3. Which words have two syllables?

   4. Which word has three syllables?

C. Make up math problems. Draw sets of shapes coming together and going away from each other. Write a story about what is happening. Use the challenge words.

Challenge Activities

trucks   sneakers   guesses   radishes

A. Read the first sentence in each pair. A challenge word is underlined. Write the form of the challenge word that means "one" to finish the second sentence.

1. These <u>radishes</u> come from our garden.
   I put a _____ in my salad.
2. My <u>sneakers</u> are old.
   The left _____ has a hole in it.
3. I gave you two <u>guesses</u>.
   Your first _____ was right.
4. We saw many <u>trucks</u> on the pike.
   One _____ was red.

B. Write a challenge word for each clue.

1. We are red and grow under the ground.
2. We help your feet feel good.
3. We move things from place to place.
4. We can be right, but we could be wrong.

C. What can trucks do? How do they help people? Write about the ideas you have. Underline any words you used that mean more than one.

A.

I.

2.

3.

4.

B.

I.

2.

3.

4.

Challenge Activities

pressed   followed   drifted   cracking

A.
1.
2.
3.
4.
B.
1.
2.
3.
4.

A. 1.–4. Write the challenge words. Circle the ending that was added to each base word.

B. Write a challenge word to finish each sentence.

1. We watched as the boat _____ across the lake.
2. We _____ a path through the woods yesterday.
3. Dan _____ his shirt after it was washed.
4. Mom is _____ eggs into a bowl.

C. Write about the picture. Use as many of the challenge words as you can.

Challenge Activities

| moose   scooter   stood   woodpecker |

A. Read each challenge word and the two words beside it. Write the word that has the same **oo** sound as the challenge word.

1. **moose**   boot   good
2. **stood**   food   took
3. **woodpecker**   book   root
4. **scooter**   noon   wool

B. Write a challenge word to finish each sentence.

1. A _____ can tap a hole in a tree.
2. A _____ is an animal in the deer family.
3. First I sat down, and then I _____ up.
4. Angie rode her _____ down the street.

C. Write about the picture. Use challenge words.

A. _____

1. _____

2. _____

3. _____

4. _____

B. _____

1. _____

2. _____

3. _____

4. _____

Challenge Activities

| says | full | pull | move |

A. Write the challenge word that has the same vowel sound as each group of words.

1. press, head, net
2. boot, pool, soon
3. wool, put, bull
4. foot, hood, took

B. Write a challenge word to complete each sentence.

1. The tub is _____ of water.
2. Bob and Lisa _____ their wagons up the hill.
3. Today we will _____ into our new house.
4. Dad always _____, "Dinner is ready!"

C. What must people do when they move to another house? Look at the picture. Make up names for the people you see. Write a story about them.

A.

1. _____

2. _____

3. _____

4. _____

B.

1. _____

2. _____

3. _____

4. _____

Challenge Activities

frown	towel	jewel	screw

A. Write the challenge word that names each picture.

1.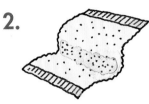

2.

3.

4.

B. Write a challenge word to finish each sentence.

1. When you're wet, you need a _____.
2. When you're angry, you might _____.
3. You should put a _____ in a safe place.
4. You can _____ in a light bulb.

C. Use the word **frown** in a sentence. Then write **noun** or **verb** to show how you have used it. Think of other words that can be nouns or verbs. Write sentences and tell whether you used the words as nouns or verbs.

A.

1.

2.

3.

4.

B.

1.

2.

3.

4.

245

ivory   orange   purple   violet

A. Answer each question about the challenge words.

1.–2. What two colors are very much alike?
3. What color is almost white?
4. What color is made by mixing red and yellow?

B. The challenge words are in the wrong sentences. Write the challenge word that belongs in each sentence.

1. The ivory tree has fruit on it.
2. The elephant's tusks are made of violet.
3. A purple is a kind of flower.
4. This grape juice is a deep orange color.

C. Copy the picture. Color the fruits and vegetables. List the colors you used.

A.

1.

2.

3.

4.

B.

1.

2.

3.

4.

Challenge Activities

| start | party | parka | scarf |

A. Write a challenge word to finish what each person says.

Welcome to the ___1.___!

Come in! The fun is about to ___2.___.

Wear this wool ___3.___.

I'll wear my ___4.___ because it's cold.

B. Each challenge word has at least two smaller words hidden in it. Write the challenge word that includes the words in each pair.

I. art, part   2. car, scar

3. ark, park   4. art, star

C. What kinds of things do you like to do at a party? Write about some of them. Use the challenge words when you can.

A.

I.

2.

3.

4.

B.

I.

2.

3.

4.

Challenge Activities

chatter	bench	wrench	whisper

A.

1.

2.

3.

4.

B.

1.

2.

3.

4.

A. 1.–2. Write the two challenge words that rhyme.

   3. Write the challenge word that rhymes with **batter**.

   4. Write the challenge word that begins like **which**.

B. Write a challenge word to finish each sentence.

   1. When you want to speak softly, you can _____.

   2. When you're cold, your teeth might _____.

   3. When you go to a park, you might sit on a _____.

   4. To fix a leaky pipe, you might use a _____.

C. The words **chatter** and **whisper** tell about two ways that people talk. What are some other words that tell about how people talk? Make a list of all the words you can think of. Then use each word or word form in a sentence.

Challenge Activities

| acorn | porch | stork | hornet |

A. Write the challenge word that goes with each picture.

1.   2.   3.   4.

B. Finish this make-believe story with challenge words.

A white __1.__ with big wings was flying in the sky. She looked down. She saw some people sitting on their front __2.__ . She saw a squirrel eating an __3.__ . Then the stork saw a mean __4.__ . "Don't you sting anybody," she called out.

C. In Part B, you read about what a stork saw while it was flying in the air. Imagine that you could fly to school from your home. What would you see on the way? How would everything look from above? Write about it. If you wish, draw a picture that shows you on your flying trip!

A.

1.

2.

3.

4.

B.

1.

2.

3.

4.

| brush | marsh | shift | shiny |

A. Write the challenge word that fits each clue.

1. bright
2. a tool for painting
3. to move or change from one place or position to another
4. soft, wet land

B. Write a challenge word to finish each sentence.

1. That new penny is _____.
2. I _____ my teeth after each meal.
3. We saw some ducks in the _____.
4. My brother works on the night _____ at his new job.

C. List things that can be made shiny. Tell how you can make one of these things shiny.

A.

1.
2.
3.
4.

B.

1.
2.
3.
4.

Challenge Activities

birth	health	thimble	thread

A. Write the challenge word that has the same beginning sound as each set of words.

   1. thin, thick, thump

   2. throw, three, thrill

Write the challenge word that has the same ending sound as each set of words.

   3. worth, girth

   4. stealth, wealth

B. Write a challenge word to finish each sentence.

   1. When she sews, Mom puts a _____ on her middle finger.

   2. Our dog gave _____ to four puppies.

   3. The _____ goes through the eye of a needle.

   4. Eating well will help you to have good _____.

C. Good health is important to everybody. What are some things people do to keep healthy? Write about them.

A.

1.

2.

3.

4.

B.

1.

2.

3.

4.

Challenge Activities

tow	reed	weak	aunt

A.

1.

2.

3.

4.

B.

1.

2.

3.

4.

A. Write a challenge word to finish each sentence.

  1. The word **ant** can sound like the word _____.

  2. The word **read** sounds like the word _____ .

  3. The word **week** sounds like the word _____.

  4. The word **toe** sounds like the word _____.

B. Write a challenge word to finish each sentence.

  1. Your mom's sister is your _____.

  2. When you don't feel strong, you feel _____.

  3. When you pull something with a rope, you _____ it.

  4. A _____ is a kind of tall grass.

C. Write four sentences. Use a challenge word or a word that sounds like a challenge word in each sentence.

Challenge Activities

dragonfly	flagpole
notebook	shoelace

A. The parts of the compound words got mixed up. Fix them by writing each challenge word correctly.

1. dragonpole
2. notelace
3. flagbook
4. shoefly

B. Write the word that goes with each picture.

1.

2.

3.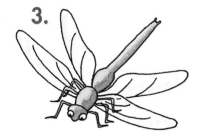

4.

C. Make a list of other compound words you know. Try to list ten words. Then use each compound word in a sentence. If you prefer, write a story and use as many of the compound words as you can.

A.

1.

2.

3.

4.

B.

1.

2.

3.

4.

WRITER'S HANDBOOK
Contents

Spelling Strategy
When You Take a Test

1 **Get** ready for the test. Make sure your paper and pencil are ready.

2 **Listen** as your teacher says each word. Listen to the sentence. Don't write before you hear the word **and** the sentence.

3 **Write** the word carefully. Make sure your printing is easy to read.

4 **Use** a pen to correct your test. Look at the word as your teacher says it.

5 **Say** the word aloud. Listen as your teacher spells the word. Say each letter. Check the word one letter at a time.

6 **Circle** any misspelled parts of the word.

7 **Look** at the correct word. Spell the word again. Say each letter out loud.

8 **Write** any misspelled word correctly.

Spelling Strategy
When You Write a Paper

1 **Think** of the word you want to use.

2 **Write** the word if you know how to spell it.

3 **Say** the word to yourself if you are not sure how to spell it.

4 **Picture** what the word looks like when it is written.

5 **Write** the word.

6 **Ask** yourself if the word looks right.

7 **Check** the dictionary if you are not sure.

SPELLING AND THE Writing Process

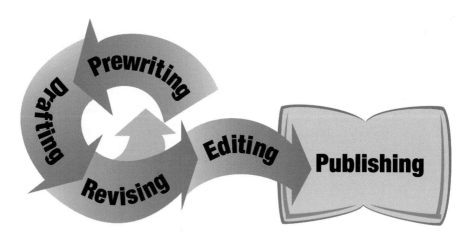

The writing process has five steps. Here is a description of each step:

Prewriting This is thinking and planning ahead to help you write.

Drafting This means writing your paper for the first time. You usually just try to get your ideas down on paper. You can fix them later.

Revising This means fixing your final draft. Here is where you rewrite, change, and add words.

Editing This is where you feel you have said all you want to say. Now you proofread your paper for spelling errors and other errors.

Publishing This is making a copy of your writing and sharing it. Put your writing in a form that your readers will enjoy.

SPELLING AND Writing Ideas

Being a good speller can help make you a more confident writer. Writing often can make you a better writer. Here are some ideas to get you started.

 ## Ideas for Descriptive Writing
You might…
- describe something very small and something very big.
- describe something from the point of view of an insect.
- describe your most prized possession.

 ## Ideas for Narrative Writing
You might…
- write a story about your first visit to someplace new.
- write a story about a bad day or a best day playing your favorite sport.

 ## Ideas for Persuasive Writing
You might…
- try to persuade your classmates to read a book you like.
- try to persuade your parents to let you have a pet.
- try to persuade your teacher to change a class rule.

 ## Ideas for Expository Writing
You might…
- write how to prepare your favorite food dish.
- inform your classmates about your pet or another favorite animal.
- write instructions on how to care for a pet.

Manuscript Handwriting Models

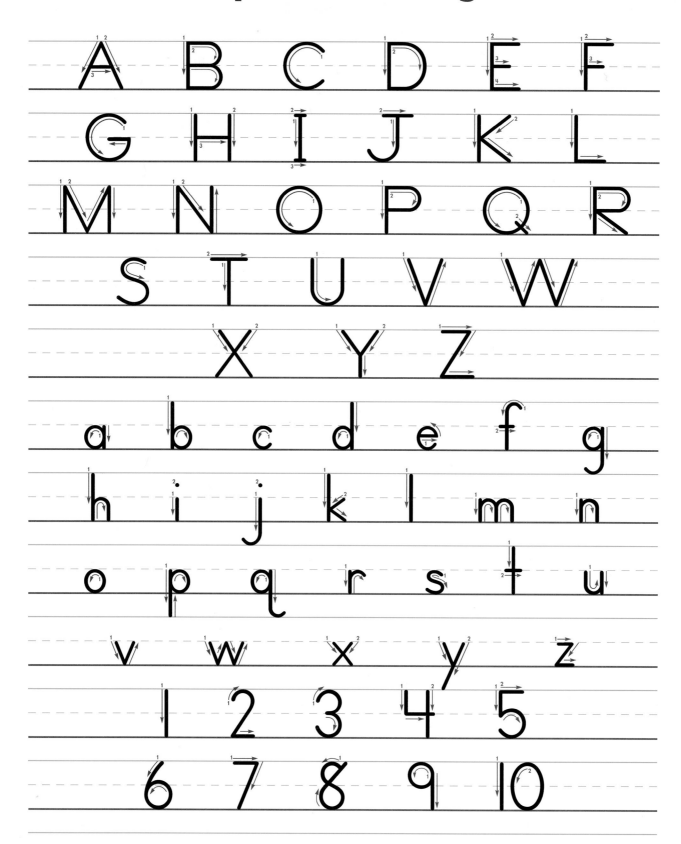

High Frequency Writing Words

A

a
about
afraid
after
again
air
all
almost
also
always
am
America
an
and
animal
animals
another
any
anything
are
around
as

ask
asked
at
ate
away

B

baby
back
bad
ball
balloons
baseball
basketball
be
bear
beautiful
because
become
bed
been
before
being

believe
best
better
big
bike
black
boat
book
books
both
boy
boys
bring
broke
brother
build
bus
but
buy
by

C

call
called
came
can
candy
can't
car
care
cars
cat
catch
caught
change
charge
children
Christmas
circus
city
class
clean
clothes
come

comes

coming

could

couldn't

country

cut

D

Dad

day

days

decided

did

didn't

died

different

dinner

do

does

doesn't

dog

dogs

doing

done

don't

door

down

dream

E

each

earth

eat

eighth

else

end

enough

even

every

everybody

everyone

everything

except

eyes

F

family

fast

father

favorite

feel

feet

fell

few

field

fight

finally

find

fire

first

fish

five

fix

food

football

for

found

four

free

Friday

friend

friends

from

front

fun

funny

future

G

game

games

gas

gave

get

gets

getting

girl

girls

give

go

God

goes

going

good

got

grade

grader
great
ground
grow

H

had
hair
half
happened
happy
hard
has
have
having
he
head
heard
help
her
here
he's
high
hill

him
his
hit
home
homework
hope
horse
horses
hot
hour
house
how
hurt

I

I
I'd
if
I'm
important
in
into
is
it

its
it's

J

job
jump
just

K

keep
kept
kids
killed
kind
knew
know

L

lady
land
last
later
learn
leave

left
let
let's
life
like
liked
likes
little
live
lived
lives
long
look
looked
looking
lost
lot
lots
love
lunch

M

mad
made

make	must	on	police
making	my	once	president
man	myself	one	pretty
many		only	probably
math	**N**	or	problem
may	name	other	put
maybe	named	our	
me	need	out	**R**
mean	never	outside	ran
men	new	over	read
might	next	own	ready
miss	nice		real
Mom	night	**P**	really
money	no	parents	reason
more	not	park	red
morning	nothing	party	responsibilities
most	now	people	rest
mother		person	ride
mouse	**O**	pick	riding
move	of	place	right
Mr.	off	planet	room
Mrs.	oh	play	rules
much	OK	played	run
music	old	playing	running

S

said
same
saw
say
scared
school
schools
sea
second
see
seen
set
seventh
she
ship
shot
should
show
sick
since
sister
sit
sleep

small
snow
so
some
someone
something
sometimes
soon
space
sport
sports
start
started
states
stay
still
stop
stopped
store
story
street
stuff
such
sudden
suddenly

summer
sure
swimming

T

take
talk
talking
teach
teacher
teachers
team
tell
than
Thanksgiving
that
that's
the
their
them
then
there
these
they
they're

thing
things
think
this
thought
three
through
throw
time
times
to
today
together
told
too
took
top
tree
trees
tried
trip
trouble
try
trying
turn

turned
TV
two

U

united
until
up
upon
us
use
used

V

very

W

walk
walked
walking
want
wanted
war
was

wasn't
watch
water
way
we
week
weeks
well
went
were
what
when
where
which
while
white
who
whole
why
will
win
winter
wish
with

without
woke
won
won't
work
world
would
wouldn't

Y

yard
year
years
yes
you
your
you're

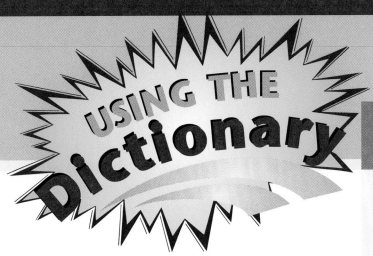

USING THE Dictionary

Tips for Finding a Word in a Dictionary

- Practice using guide words in a dictionary. Think of words to spell. Then use the guide words to find each word's entry. Do this again and again until you can use guide words easily.

- Some spellings are listed with the base word. To find **nicest,** you would look up **nice**. To find **chopped,** you would look up **chop**. To find **pennies,** you would look up **penny.**

- If you do not know how to spell a word, guess the spelling. Try to find the first three letters of the word. (If you just use the first letter, you will probably take too long.)

- If you can't find a word, think of how else it might be spelled. For example, if a word starts with the **/k/ sound,** the spelling might begin with **k** or **c.**

Guide Words

The **guide words** at the top of each dictionary page can help you find the word you want quickly. The first guide word tells you the first word on that page. The second guide word tells you the last word on that page. The entries on the page fall in a-b-c order between these two guide words.

Entries

Words you want to find in the dictionary are called **entries**. Entries tell a lot besides the correct spelling. Look at the sample entry below.

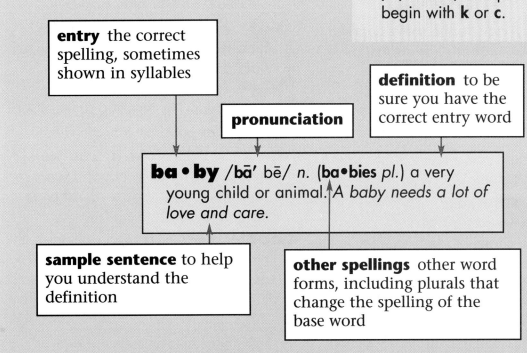

entry the correct spelling, sometimes shown in syllables

pronunciation

definition to be sure you have the correct entry word

ba•by /bā′ bē/ *n.* (ba•bies *pl.*) a very young child or animal. *A baby needs a lot of love and care.*

sample sentence to help you understand the definition

other spellings other word forms, including plurals that change the spelling of the base word

add /ăd/ *v.* to join to make something larger. *If you add 3 and 2, you get 5.*

all¹ /ôl/ *adj.* each one of. *All the books are here.*

all² /ôl/ *adv.* entirely. *Our milk is all gone.*

an•y /ĕn′ ē/ *adj.* **a.** one out of a group. *Read any book you like.* **b.** some. *Would you like any orange juice?*

ap•ple /ăp′ əl/ *n.* a fruit for eating that grows on a tree. *Apples may be red, green, or yellow.*

arm /ärm/ *n.* the part of the body between the shoulder and the hand. *To raise your hand, you must lift your arm.*

art /ärt/ *n.* writing, painting, music, etc. *We are drawing pictures for our art show.*

as /ăz/ *adv.* to the same degree; equally. *Tom can run as fast as I can.*

ask /ăsk/ *v.* to try to find out or get by using words. *Let's ask Mr. Fulton how to get there.*

ate /āt/ *v.* past tense of **eat**. *She ate a banana.*

ax or **axe** /ăks/ *n.* (**ax•es** *pl.*) a tool with a sharp blade fastened to a handle. *We split firewood with an ax.*

ax

ba•by /bā′ bē/ *n.* (**ba•bies** *pl.*) a very young child or animal. *A baby needs a lot of love and care.*

ball /bôl/ *n.* **a.** a toy for throwing or kicking. *Catch the ball!* **b.** something round. *The cat loves to play with a ball of yarn.*

bank¹ /băngk/ *n.* the ground at the edge of a lake or river. *Can you swim to the bank?*

bank² /băngk/ *n.* a place where people may keep or borrow money. *Do you have an account at the bank?*

base /bās/ *n.* a starting or resting place. *Robert ran around the field, then back to the base.*

base•ball /bās′ bôl/ *n.* a game played with a bat and a ball by two teams of nine players each. *Debbie wants to play baseball.*

bat¹ /băt/ *n.* a heavy stick used to hit a ball. *Mike showed me how to hold the bat.*

bat² /băt/ *v.* (**bats, bat•ted, bat•ting**) to hit. *She batted the ball out of the park for a home run.*

be /bē/ *v.* (**am, are, is, was, were, been, be•ing**) **a.** to equal. *I want to be a hero.* **b.** to happen. *When is the game going to be?*

bean /bēn/ *n.* a seed or pod that can be eaten as a vegetable. *We ate green beans for lunch.*

bed•room /bĕd′ rŏŏm′/ *n.* a room used for sleeping. *We have bunk beds in our bedroom.*

beef /bēf/ *n.* the meat of a cow or steer. *We had beef, carrots, and peas for supper.*

been /bĭn/ *v.* a form of **be**. *She has been a teacher for twenty years.*

bell /bĕl/ *n.* a hollow piece of metal that makes a ringing sound when struck. *The bell in the tower rings every hour.*

bill[1] /bĭl/ *n.* **a.** a statement of money owed. *The doctor sent a bill for my shots.* **b.** a piece of paper money. *I found a dollar bill.*

bill[2] /bĭl/ *n.* the beak of a bird. *Ducks have wide, flat bills.*

bird /bûrd/ *n.* an animal that has feathers and wings. *Almost all birds can fly.*

birth•day /bûrth′ dā′/ *n.* the day one was born, or the same date in another year. *Rosa and I have the same birthday.*

black /blăk/ *n.* the darkest color. *These words are printed in black.*

blew /blōō/ *v.* past tense of **blow**. *I blew out the candle.*

▶ **Blew** sounds like **blue**.

blow /blō/ *v.* (**blows, blew, blown, blow•ing**) to move, drive, or force by air. *Make a wish and blow out the candles.*

blue /blōō/ *n.* the color of the sky on a clear day. *Blue is her favorite color.*

▶ **Blue** sounds like **blew**.

Pronunciation Key

ă	pat	ŏ	pot	th	**th**in
ā	pay	ō	toe	*th*	**th**is
âr	care	ô	paw, for	hw	**wh**ich
ä	father	oi	noise	zh	vi**s**ion
ĕ	pet	ou	out	ə	**a**bout,
ē	be	ŏŏ	took		item,
ĭ	pit	ōō	boot		pencil,
ī	pie	ŭ	cut		gallop,
îr	pier	ûr	urge		circus

boat /bōt/ *n.* a small vessel for traveling on water. *The boat sailed across the lake.*

book /bŏŏk/ *n.* written or printed sheets of paper put together inside a cover. *That book has a red jacket.*

book

boot /bōōt/ *n.* a cover for the foot and leg. *Sean and I have rubber boots.*

born /bôrn/ *adj.* brought into life. *A new baby was born next door.*

both /bōth/ *adj.* the two. *Tell me both ways to get to school.*

bounce /bouns/ *v.* (**bounc•es, bounced, bounc•ing**) to hit against a surface and spring back. *The rubber ball bounced off the wall.*

box /bŏks/ *n.* (**box•es** *pl.*) a case for holding things. *Please put the tools back in the box.*

boy /boi/ *n.* a male child. *We have only one boy in our family.*

bring /brĭng/ *v.* (**brings, brought, bring•ing**) to carry from somewhere else. *Please bring my book with you.*

brown /broun/ *n.* the color of chocolate. *Brown is the color of my hair.*

bulb /bŭlb/ *n.* **a.** the round underground stem of certain plants. *Onions and tulips grow from bulbs.* **b.** a glass globe that gives off light. *The lamp needs a new bulb.*

bush /bo͝osh/ *n.* (**bush•es** *pl.*) a small tree; a shrub. *A rose grows on a bush.*

but•ter•fly /bŭt′ ər flī′/ *n.* (**but•ter•flies** *pl.*) an insect with four big brightly colored wings. *Is that a moth or a butterfly?*

by /bī/ *prep.* **a.** near. *Stay by her.* **b.** along. *We came home by the old road.* **c.** through the effort of. *The project was done by the second grade class.*

cake /kāk/ *n.* a sweet, bread-like food made from batter. *The cake is mixed and ready to bake.*

cake

call[1] /kôl/ *v.* to shout; to cry out. *Did Lani hear you call her?*

call[2] /kôl/ *n.* a cry. *That bird's call sounds like a whistle.*

can•not /kăn′ ŏt/ or /kə nŏt′/ *v.* is or are not able to. *They cannot come with us.*

cap /kăp/ *n.* a small hat that fits closely on the head. *How do you like my baseball cap?*

car /kär/ *n.* an automobile. *We went for a ride in the car.*

car•toon /kär to͞on′/ *n.* a funny drawing or movie. *We love the cartoons in the Sunday paper.*

cash[1] /kăsh/ *n.* money in coins and bills. *I have two dollars in cash.*

cash[2] /kăsh/ *v.* (**cash•es, cashed, cash•ing**) to exchange for money. *The bank will cash this check.*

cave /kāv/ *n.* a hollow space that goes into the earth. *They found a fossil inside the cave.*

chalk /chôk/ *n.* a soft mineral used for writing or drawing. *It's fun to use colored chalk on the board.*

chill[1] /chĭl/ *n.* coldness. *There is a chill in the air.*

chill[2] /chĭl/ *v.* to make cool. *Did you chill the fruit juice?*

chin /chĭn/ *n.* the part of the face beneath the bottom lip. *You move your chin when you chew.*

chirp[1] /chûrp/ *n.* a short, sharp sound made by some insects and animals. *Listen to the chirp of the crickets.*

chirp[2] /chûrp/ *v.* to make a short, sharp sound. *Some sparrows chirp.*

chop /chŏp/ *v.* (**chops, chopped, chop•ping**) to cut by hitting with a sharp tool like an ax. *We need to chop wood for our campfire.*

clam /klăm/ *n.* a shellfish that can be eaten steamed or fried. *Clams live in sand along the ocean coasts.*

clap¹ /klăp/ *v.* (**claps, clapped, clap•ping**) to strike the hands together. *After the play we all began to clap.*

clap² /klăp/ *n.* a sudden loud noise or crash. *I heard a clap of thunder.*

class /klăs/ *n.* (**class•es** *pl.*) a group of students learning together. *There are more boys than girls in my class.*

clean¹ /klēn/ *adj.* free from dirt. *Put on clean clothes for the party.*

clean² /klēn/ *v.* to make clean. *Dad made me clean my room.*

clown /kloun/ *n.* a person who dresses up and acts funny to make us laugh. *The clown drove a tiny car in the parade.*

clown

club /klŭb/ *n.* **a.** a heavy stick used in playing games. *She hit the golf ball with her club.* **b.** a group of people meeting together. *I want to join the stamp club.*

coat /kōt/ *n.* an outer garment with sleeves. *In winter I wear a heavy coat over my other clothes.*

co•coon /kə koōn'/ *n.* the silk covering that a caterpillar makes and lives in. *When the cocoon opens, the caterpillar comes out as a butterfly or a moth.*

coin /koin/ *n.* a piece of metal money. *Pennies, nickels, dimes, and quarters are coins.*

Pronunciation Key

ă	pat	ŏ	pot	th	**th**in
ā	pay	ō	toe	*th*	**th**is
âr	care	ô	paw, for	hw	**wh**ich
ä	father	oi	noise	zh	vi**s**ion
ĕ	pet	ou	out	ə	**a**bout,
ē	be	oŏ	took		item,
ĭ	pit	oō	boot		pencil,
ī	pie	ŭ	cut		gallop,
îr	pier	ûr	urge		circus

cold¹ /kōld/ *adj.* having a low temperature; not warm. *January is a cold month.*

cold² /kōld/ *n.* a common illness. *Drink lots of orange juice when you have a cold.*

col•or¹ /kŭl' ər/ *n.* a bright or dark shade caused by the effect of light rays on the eyes. *Purple is her favorite color.*

col•or² /kŭl' ər/ *v.* to change the color. *Color the stars yellow.*

come /kŭm/ *v.* (**comes, came, come, com•ing**) **a.** to move toward. *Come over to my house.* **b.** to happen. *Your birthday comes once a year.*

cook¹ /koŏk/ *v.* to prepare food for eating by using heat. *Broiling is one way to cook food.*

cook² /koŏk/ *n.* a person who prepares food. *Everybody likes the cook at our school.*

cord /kôrd/ *n.* **a.** heavy string. *The big package was tied with cord.* **b.** a covered electrical wire. *A worn cord can cause a fire.*

corn /kôrn/ *n.* a grain that grows in kernels or seeds on large ears. *We ate corn and peas for dinner.*

corn

cot /kŏt/ *n.* a light bed that can be folded up. *Many cots are made of canvas on a metal or wood frame.*

count /kount/ *v.* **a.** to name the numbers in order. *Our baby is learning to count already.* **b.** to add to find the total. *He counted the quarters in his bank.*

cow /kou/ *n.* a large farm animal that gives milk. *Our cow just had a calf.*

crab /krăb/ *n.* a shellfish with a broad, flat body, eight legs, and two claws. *We ate fresh ocean crabs for supper.*

cry¹ /krī/ *v.* (**cries, cried, cry•ing**) to weep; to shed tears. *We heard the baby cry.*

cry² /krī/ *n.* (**cries** pl.) the sound made by an animal. *We woke up to the cry of the bird.*

cup /kŭp/ *n.* a small, hollow container used for drinking. *Pour some milk into my cup, please.*

cute /kyo͞ot/ *adj.* (**cut•er, cut•est**) pretty; attractive. *We saw a cute puppy at the pet shop.*

dark¹ /därk/ *adj.* not light; having little or no light. *I like to look at stars on a clear, dark night.*

dark² /därk/ *n.* darkness; nightfall. *You must return before dark.*

dash¹ /dăsh/ *v.* (**dash•es, dashed, dash•ing**) to rush quickly. *We dashed to the store, but it had closed.*

dash² /dăsh/ *n.* (**dash•es** pl.) **a.** a mark (—) used to show a break or pause. *A dash causes a complete stop—like this.* **b.** a small amount. *Add a dash of pepper.*

day /dā/ *n.* **a.** the time between sunrise and sunset. *We traveled during the day and slept at night.* **b.** a period of twenty-four hours. *A week has seven days.*

dear /dîr/ *adj.* greatly loved. *She gave the book to a dear friend.*

▶ **Dear** sounds like **deer**.

deer /dîr/ *n.* (**deer** pl.) a graceful animal with hooves. *The male deer has antlers.*

▶ **Deer** sounds like **dear**.

den • tal /dĕn′ tl/ *adj.* of or for the teeth. *Brush your teeth after every meal for good dental health.*

den • tist /dĕn′ tĭst/ *n.* a doctor who takes care of the teeth. *The dentist told me that I had no cavities.*

dime /dīm/ *n.* a silver coin used as money by the United States and Canada. *A dime is worth ten cents.*

dish¹ /dĭsh/ *n.* (**dish•es** pl.) a container for holding food. *Put the peas in a big dish.*

dish² /dĭsh/ *v.* to put food into a serving dish. *Todd, please dish up the applesauce.*

do /dōo/ v. (**does, did, done, do•ing**) **a.** to perform or carry out a job. *Will you please do the dishes?* **b.** to act or behave. *You are doing very well.*

doc • tor /dŏc′ tər/ n. a person trained to prevent and heal diseases. *See your doctor for a regular checkup.*

does /dŭz/ v. a form of **do**. *Tim does neat work.*

dog /dôg/ or /dŏg/ n. a four-legged animal that makes a good pet. *Some dogs watch houses or tend sheep.*

doll /dŏl/ n. a toy that looks like a person. *The doll I like best has a lot of different clothes.*

done /dŭn/ v. a form of **do**. *Have you done your math homework yet?*

don • key /dŏng′ kē/ n. an animal like a horse, but smaller and with longer ears. *A donkey is a strong work animal.*

door /dôr/ or /dōr/ n. a movable part that can be opened and closed to form an entrance. *Open the door and go in.*

down¹ /doun/ adv. from a high place or position to a lower one. *The airplane came down for a landing.*

down² /doun/ n. soft feathers. *The baby birds were covered with down.*

down • town /doun′ toun′/ adv. in or toward the main business part of a city. *We all went downtown to shop.*

Pronunciation Key

ă	pat	ŏ	pot	th	**th**in
ā	pay	ō	toe	th	**th**is
âr	care	ô	paw, for	hw	**wh**ich
ä	father	oi	noise	zh	vi**s**ion
ĕ	pet	ou	out	ə	**a**bout,
ē	be	ŏŏ	took		item,
ĭ	pit	ōō	boot		pencil,
ī	pie	ŭ	cut		gallop,
îr	pier	ûr	urge		circus

drank /drăngk/ v. past tense of **drink**. *Bill drank a glass of water.*

dress¹ /drĕs/ n. (**dress•es** pl.) an outer garment with a skirt. *Judy has a plaid dress.*

dress² /drĕs/ v. (**dress•es, dressed, dress•ing**) to put clothes on. *Can you dress in five minutes?*

drink¹ /drĭngk/ v. (**drinks, drank, drunk, drink•ing**) to take a liquid into the mouth and swallow it. *Do you drink much milk?*

drink² /drĭngk/ n. liquid that is swallowed. *May I have a drink of water?*

drive¹ /drīv/ v. (**drives, drove, driv•en, driv•ing**) to make a car or working animal go. *Who is going to drive me home?*

drive² /drīv/ n. a trip in a car. *We took a drive last Sunday.*

drum /drŭm/ n. a musical instrument that makes a sound when beaten. *The marchers kept time to the beat of a drum.*

drum

dry¹ /drī/ adj. (**dri•er, dri•est**) not wet or moist. *The ground was dry before the rain came.*

dry² /drī/ v. (**dries, dried, dry•ing**) to make or become dry. *Please dry the dishes.*

dust¹ /dŭst/ n. a light powder of dirt. *I could see the dust on the old table.*

dust² /dŭst/ v. to remove dust by wiping. *He dusted the books in the bookcase.*

each /ēch/ adj. every one in a larger group. *Each child wore a nametag.*

eat /ēt/ v. (**eats, ate, eat•en, eat•ing**) **a.** to take food into the mouth, chew it, and swallow it. *We eat beans for lunch.* **b.** to have a meal. *Did you eat yet?*

egg /ĕg/ n. the rounded container in which a baby bird grows. *Our hens lay many eggs.*

egg

eight /āt/ n. the next number after seven; seven plus one; 8. *She will turn eight next week.*

end¹ /ĕnd/ n. the point at which something either begins or stops. *A piece of string has two ends.*

end² /ĕnd/ v. to finish. *I didn't like the way the story ended.*

fall /fôl/ v. (**falls, fell, fall•en, fall•ing**) to drop from a higher place. *Leaves fall from trees.*

fan¹ /făn/ n. anything used to move the air. *When it got hot I turned on the fan.*

fan² /făn/ v. (**fans, fanned, fan•ning**) to stir up air. *A breeze fanned the room.*

far /fär/ adj. a long way off; distant. *The school is far from my house, so I leave very early.*

farm /färm/ n. the land used for growing crops or for raising animals. *My uncle raises wheat on his farm in Kansas.*

fat¹ /făt/ n. a greasy substance in animals and plants. *I trim the fat from my meat.*

fat² /făt/ adj. having much flesh; plump. *Those cows are fat.*

fawn /fôn/ n. a young deer. *A fawn's spots make it hard to see in the woods.*

fell /fĕl/ v. past tense of **fall**. *Brad fell and scraped his knee.*

fif•ty /fĭf' tē/ n. five times ten; 50. *Our flag has fifty stars.*

fill /fĭl/ v. to put as much as you can into; to make full. *Mom is filling the goldfish bowl.*

fine¹ /fīn/ adj. good; excellent. *Today is a fine day for a picnic.*

fine[2] /fīn/ *n.* money paid for breaking a rule. *I paid a fine because my library book was overdue.*

fin•ger•nail /fĭng′ gər nāl′/ *n.* a hard, thin layer at the end of each finger. *I keep my fingernails short to play the piano.*

fire /fīr/ *n.* flame; heat and light caused by burning. *The campers made a fire at night.*

first[1] /fûrst/ *adj.* before the others. *Tomorrow is the first day of spring.*

first[2] /fûrst/ *adv.* before any others. *Dee arrived first.*

fit[1] /fĭt/ *v.* (**fits, fit** or **fit•ted, fit•ting**) to be right for. *My new shoes fit my feet.*

fit[2] /fĭt/ *adj.* in good condition. *My sister is running to get fit.*

five /fīv/ *n.* one more than four; 5. *I got all five right.*

flag /flăg/ *n.* **a.** a piece of cloth with colors and designs that stand for something. *Our scout troop has a flag.* **b.** a piece of cloth used as a signal. *A red flag may mean danger.*

flat /flăt/ *adj.* (**flat•ter, flat•test**) level and even. *The tabletop is flat.*

flew /flōō/ *v.* past tense of **fly**. *The birds flew south last winter.*

floss /flôs/ or /flŏs/ *n.* a smooth, shiny thread. *The dentist said I should use floss to clean my teeth.*

fly[1] /flī/ *v.* (**flies, flew, fly•ing**) **a.** to move through the air by using wings. *Birds fly.* **b.** to travel by air. *This summer we will fly to Dallas.*

Pronunciation Key

ă	pat	ŏ	pot	th	**th**in
ā	pay	ō	toe	*th*	**th**is
âr	care	ô	paw, for	hw	**wh**ich
ä	father	oi	noise	zh	vi**s**ion
ĕ	pet	ou	**ou**t	ə	**a**bout,
ē	be	ŏŏ	t**oo**k		item,
ĭ	pit	ōō	b**oo**t		pencil,
ī	pie	ŭ	cut		gall**o**p,
îr	p**ier**	ûr	**ur**ge		circ**u**s

fly[2] /flī/ *n.* (**flies** *pl.*) an insect with two wings. *Can you swat that fly?*

fly

foal /fōl/ *n.* a young horse or donkey. *The foal ran beside its mother.*

fog /fôg/ or /fŏg/ *n.* a cloud near the surface of the land; heavy mist. *Fog is made of tiny drops of water.*

food /fōōd/ *n.* anything taken in by plants and animals that makes them live and grow. *Spinach is a healthy food.*

foot /fŏŏt/ *n.* (**feet** *pl.*) **a.** the part of the body at the end of the leg. *Start the dance with your left foot.* **b.** a measure of length. *Twelve inches make a foot.*

foot•ball /fŏŏt′ bôl′/ *n.* a game played by throwing, kicking, and running with a ball. *Wear your helmet when you play football.*

foot•step /fŏŏt′ stĕp′/ *n.* the sound made by a person walking. *We heard footsteps coming up the sidewalk.*

for /fôr/ *prep.* **a.** with the purpose of. *We are going for a bike ride.* **b.** sent or given to. *This letter is for you.* **c.** because of. *We jumped for joy.*

fork /fôrk/ *n.* a pointed tool used for lifting food or hay. *You can't eat soup with a fork.*

four /fôr/ or /fōr/ *n.* one more than three; 4. *We need four to play this game.*

fourth¹ /fôrth/ or /fōrth/ *adj.* next after the third. *I am the fourth one in line.*

fourth² /fôrth/ or /fōrth/ *n.* one of four equal parts. *A quarter is a fourth of a dollar.*

fox /fŏks/ *n.* (**fox•es** *pl.*) a wild animal like a dog but with a bushy tail. *A fox may live in a den.*

fox

free /frē/ *adj.* **a.** loose; not tied down. *We tried to catch the free end of the dog's leash.* **b.** not costing anything. *Our neighbor gave us free tickets.*

from /frŭm/ *prep.* **a.** out of. *We live thirty miles from town.* **b.** beginning with. *The party will last from two to four.*

front /frŭnt/ *n.* **a.** a part that faces forward. *The front of the house faces the street.* **b.** the first part. *The pilot sits in the front of the plane.*

frost /frôst/ or /frŏst/ *n.* **a.** frozen dew or moisture. *In cold weather our windows have frost on them.* **b.** cold weather. *Frost can hurt a crop of fruit trees.*

fry /frī/ *v.* (**fries, fried, fry•ing**) to cook in hot oil over direct heat. *Fry these vegetables lightly to keep them crisp.*

gar • den /gär′ dn/ *n.* a piece of ground in which vegetables or flowers are grown. *Rabbits ate some of the lettuce in our garden.*

gi • ant¹ /jī′ ənt/ *n.* an imaginary person of great size and strength. *The giant in the story can walk a mile in one step.*

gi • ant² /jī′ ənt/ *adj.* very big; huge. *Look at those giant trees!*

girl /gûrl/ *n.* a female child. *Their new baby is a girl.*

give /gĭv/ *v.* (**gives, gave, giv•en, giv•ing**) to hand over; to let have. *I will give this game to Ernesto.*

glad /glăd/ *adj.* **a.** happy; pleased. *We are glad that you could come.* **b.** willing, ready. *He will be glad to help you.*

glass /glăs/ *n.* (**glass•es** *pl.*) **a.** a hard substance that can be seen through. *Glass is used in windows.* **b.** a container for drinking. *Please hand me a water glass.*

Spelling Dictionary

go /gō/ *v.* **(goes, went, gone, go•ing) a.** to get to another place. *Let's go to your house.* **b.** to work or run. *The car won't go.*

good /good/ *adj.* **(bet•ter, best) a.** of high quality; better than the usual kind. *I saw a good movie last night.* **b.** well-behaved. *Our teacher says that we are a good class.*

grade /grād/ *n.* **a.** class or year in school. *The fifth grade is in room 210.* **b.** a slope in a road. *The road up the mountain has a steep grade.*

grain /grān/ *n.* the seeds of a cereal plant such as wheat, oats, or corn. *I like bread made with whole grains.*

grape /grāp/ *n.* a small, sweet fruit that grows in bunches on a vine. *Raisins are dried grapes.*

grass /grăs/ *n.* a plant with thin leaves, found in lawns or pastures. *He will mow the grass.*

gray /grā/ *n.* color made by mixing black and white. *Gray is a good color for our fence.*

green /grēn/ *n.* the color of growing grass and many other plants. *In a rainbow, green is between blue and yellow.*

grew /groo/ *v.* past tense of **grow**. *I grew a bean plant.*

group /groop/ *n.* a number of persons or things together. *A group of children stood on the corner waiting for the bus.*

Pronunciation Key

ă	pat	ŏ	pot	th	**thin**
ā	pay	ō	toe	*th*	**th**is
âr	care	ô	paw, for	hw	**wh**ich
ä	father	oi	noise	zh	vision
ĕ	pet	ou	**out**	ə	**a**bout,
ē	be	oo	took		item,
ĭ	pit	oo	boot		pencil,
ī	pie	ŭ	cut		gallop,
îr	pier	ûr	urge		circus

grow /grō/ *v.* **(grows, grew, grown, grow•ing) a.** to become larger; to increase. *Our baby is growing so fast!* **b.** to live in a certain place. *Palm trees grow in the tropics.* **c.** to raise by planting seeds and caring for. *We grow tomatoes in our garden.*

guess[1] /gĕs/ *v.* **(guess•es, guessed, guess•ing)** to form an opinion without being sure. *When I forgot my watch, I had to guess the time.*

guess[2] /gĕs/ *n.* **(guess•es** *pl.*) an opinion formed without being sure. *That was a good guess.*

gum /gŭm/ *n.* the pink, firm flesh above and below the teeth. *Healthy teeth need healthy gums.*

ham • mer[1] /hăm' ər/ *n.* a tool for pounding. *A carpenter uses a heavy hammer.*

hammer

ham•mer² /hăm' ər/ v. to pound. *Hammer this nail into the wood.*

hand /hănd/ n. the part of the arm below the wrist. *I write with my left hand.*

hang /hăng/ v. (**hangs, hung, hang•ing**) **a.** to fasten or be fastened from above. *Let's hang the wash on the line.* **b.** to droop; bend down. *The branches hang down after the heavy snowfall.*

hard¹ /härd/ adj. **a.** not soft. *Ice is hard.* **b.** not easy. *That ball was hard to catch.*

hard² /härd/ adv. with effort. *We worked hard for the team.*

harm¹ /härm/ n. injury; hurt; damage. *The storm did a lot of harm to the trees.*

harm² /härm/ v. to damage; to hurt or injure. *Poor eating habits can harm your health.*

have /hăv/ v. (**has, had, hav•ing**) **a.** to own; to possess. *They have a new house.* **b.** to cause to. *Have him play another song.* **c.** to accept; to take. *Have an apple.* **d.** to experience. *I hope he had a nice time.*

hay /hā/ n. grass that is cut and dried for use as food for animals. *Cows eat hay in the winter.*

hay

head /hĕd/ n. **a.** the part of the body that contains the eyes, ears, nose, and mouth. *Don't bump your head.* **b.** the top or front part. *I was at the head of the line.*

hear /hîr/ v. (**hears, heard, hear•ing**) **a.** to take in sound with the ears. *I hear a funny noise.* **b.** to listen to. *We like to hear good music.*

▶ **Hear** sounds like **here**.

heel /hēl/ n. the rounded part at the back of the foot. *I stepped on a rock and hurt my heel.*

help¹ /hĕlp/ v. to aid; to assist. *Please help me wash the dog.*

help² /hĕlp/ n. the act of doing what is useful. *Sarah gave me some help with my homework.*

help•er /hĕl' pər/ n. one who helps. *Dad says I'm a good helper.*

her¹ /hûr/ adj. of or belonging to a girl or woman. *Donna lost her key.*

her² /hûr/ pron. that girl or woman. *Rosa took the bag with her.*

here /hîr/ adv. **a.** in or at this place. *We like living here.* **b.** to or into this place. *Please come here.*

▶ **Here** sounds like **hear**.

hill /hĭl/ n. land that is higher than the land around it, but not so tall as a mountain. *From the top of the hill, we could see for miles.*

hit /hĭt/ v. (**hits, hit, hit•ting**) to give a blow to; to strike. *Chris hit the ball over the net.*

hoe¹ /hō/ n. a digging tool with a thin, flat blade and a long handle. *Hoes are used for loosening soil.*

hoe² /hō/ v. (**hoes, hoed, hoe•ing**) to dig with a hoe. *Robin hoes her garden every day.*

Spelling Dictionary

hold /hōld/ v. (**holds, held, hold•ing**) **a.** to take and not let go. *I was asked to hold the baby.* **b.** to keep in a certain position. *Hold your head high.*

horse /hôrs/ n. a large, hoofed animal used for riding and pulling loads. *A colt is a young horse.*

hour /our/ n. **a.** sixty minutes. *There are twenty-four hours in a day.* **b.** a certain time. *The doctor's office hours are from ten to four.*

▶ **Hour** sounds like **our**.

how /hou/ adv. **a.** in what way. *How do you boil an egg?* **b.** to what degree or amount. *How hot is it outside?* **c.** in what condition. *They asked me how I felt.*

hung /hŭng/ v. past tense of **hang**. *Jay hung his coat on a hook.*

hunt /hŭnt/ v. to search; to try to find. *We all hunted for the lost ball.*

ill /ĭl/ adj. not healthy; sick. *Julie stayed home when she was ill.*

inch /ĭnch/ n. (**inch•es** pl.) a measure of length. *Twelve inches are one foot.*

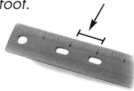

inch

Pronunciation Key

ă	pat	ŏ	pot	th	**th**in
ā	p**ay**	ō	t**oe**	th	**th**is
âr	c**are**	ô	p**aw, for**	hw	**wh**ich
ä	f**a**ther	oi	n**oi**se	zh	vi**si**on
ĕ	pet	ou	**ou**t	ə	**a**bout,
ē	be	ŏŏ	t**oo**k		it**e**m,
ĭ	pit	ōō	b**oo**t		penc**i**l,
ī	p**ie**	ŭ	c**u**t		gall**o**p,
îr	p**ier**	ûr	**ur**ge		circ**u**s

in•side¹ /ĭn sīd′/ or /ĭn′ sīd′/ adv. within; not outside. *When it rains we play inside.*

in•side² /ĭn sīd′/ or /ĭn′ sīd′/ adj. inner. *My jacket has an inside pocket.*

in•to /ĭn′ tōō/ prep. **a.** to the inside of. *She walked into the room.* **b.** to the form of. *Water turns into ice in cold weather.*

jaw /jô/ n. the lowest part of the face; the part that holds the teeth. *When you yawn, your jaw drops.*

joke /jōk/ n. something said or done to make someone laugh. *Rob told a funny joke.*

jug /jŭg/ n. a big bottle with a narrow mouth. *They brought a jug of milk from the farm.*

jump /jŭmp/ v. to leap off the ground. *It was fun to watch the horses jump over the fences.*

junk /jŭngk/ n. worthless or useless goods; trash. *We threw out all of the junk from our garage.*

Spelling Dictionary

just¹ /jŭst/ *adj.* fair; honest. *That was the only just way to decide.*

just² /jŭst/ *adv.* **a.** exactly. *You did that just right!* **b.** a short time ago. *I just saw her there.* **c.** only. *We get just one turn at bat.*

kick¹ /kĭk/ *v.* to hit with the foot. *The restless horse kicked the stall.*

kick² /kĭk/ *n.* a blow made by the foot. *Marika gave the ball a hard kick.*

king /kĭng/ *n.* **a.** the male ruler of a country. *Some kings wear crowns.* **b.** a person or thing best in its class. *The lion is known as the king of the jungle.*

kiss¹ /kĭs/ *v.* (**kiss•es, kissed, kiss•ing**) to touch with the lips as a sign of love or greeting. *The girl kissed her mother and left for camp.*

kiss

kiss² /kĭs/ *n.* (**kiss•es** *pl.*) a touch of the lips. *His aunt gave him a kiss.*

know /nō/ *v.* (**knows, knew, known, know•ing**) **a.** to understand; have knowledge about. *Do you know how to knit?* **b.** to be aware of; realize. *I didn't know they had moved away.*

late /lāt/ *adj.* (**lat•er, lat•est; late•ly,** *adv.*) **a.** happening after the usual time. *I was late for school.* **b.** near the end of a certain time. *It's too late to shop.*

leap /lēp/ *v.* (**leaps, leaped** or **leapt, leap•ing**) to jump or spring. *The horse leaped over the fence.*

li•on /lī' ən/ *n.* a large, powerful, brownish-yellow member of the cat family. *A group of lions is called a pride.*

lit•ter /lĭt' ər/ *n.* **a.** loose trash or rubbish. *There was a lot of litter in the park.* **b.** a number of baby animals born at one time. *The cat had a litter of kittens.*

live¹ /lĭv/ *v.* (**lives, lived, liv•ing**) **a.** to have one's home; to reside; dwell. *Theo lives on Camden Street.* **b.** to be alive; to have life. *Most plants need sun to live.*

live² /līv/ *adj.* alive; having life. *We saw a live parrot at the zoo.*

lob•ster /lŏb' stər/ *n.* a shellfish with two big claws and eight legs. *There were live lobsters in the tank at the restaurant.*

lock¹ /lŏk/ *n.* a device for fastening a door, drawer, etc. *Do you have a key that will fit this lock?*

lock² /lŏk/ *v.* to fasten with a lock. *Lock the door when you go out.*

log /lôg/ or /lŏg/ *n.* a long piece of a tree that has been cut down. *Logs are cut into smaller pieces for building and for firewood.*

long /lông/ or /lŏng/ *adj.*
a. having great distance or length of time. *It's a long walk to the bus stop.* **b.** having a certain length. *The room is twelve feet long.*

look /lo͝ok/ *v.* **a.** to use or turn the eyes in order to see. *Look both ways before you cross the street.* **b.** to search. *We looked all over for my library book.*

loom /lo͞om/ *n.* a machine for weaving cloth out of thread. *A weaver uses both hands and feet to work a loom.*

lot /lŏt/ *n.* a large amount; many. *We have a lot of books in our room.*

low /lō/ *adj.* **a.** not high; not tall. *A skyscraper is tall; most houses are low.* **b.** soft; not loud. *The kitten gave a low purr.*

luck /lŭk/ *n.* good fortune. *We had the luck to get the best seats.*

man•y /mĕn' ē/ *adj.* (**more, most**) a great number of. *Many children were late to school because of the snow.*

map¹ /măp/ *n.* a flat picture or chart of a part of the surface of the earth. *Maps show where to find towns, rivers, and roads.*

map

Pronunciation Key

ă	pat	ŏ	pot	th	**th**in
ā	pay	ō	toe	th	**th**is
âr	care	ô	paw, for	hw	**wh**ich
ä	father	oi	noise	zh	vi**s**ion
ĕ	pet	ou	out	ə	**a**bout,
ē	be	o͝o	took		item,
ĭ	pit	o͞o	boot		pencil,
ī	pie	ŭ	cut		gallop,
îr	pier	ûr	urge		circus

map² /măp/ *v.* (**maps, mapped, map•ping**) to plan using a map. *Let's map out the path we will take.*

match¹ /măch/ *v.* (**match•es, matched, match•ing**) to be the same as; to go with. *Does this block match the other one?*

match² /măch/ *n.* (**match•es** *pl.*) a piece of wood or cardboard that bursts into flame when it is scratched. *A match won't light if it's wet.*

may /mā/ *v.* (**might**) **a.** to be allowed to. *May I be excused?* **b.** to be likely to. *It may snow this morning.*

maze /māz/ *n.* a set of paths built so they are hard to follow. *To solve this puzzle you must trace the right path through the maze.*

meat /mēt/ *n.* the flesh of an animal used as food. *My favorite meat is turkey.*

▶ **Meat** sounds like **meet**.

meet /mēt/ v. (**meets, met, meet•ing**) **a.** to come face to face with; to come together. *I'll meet you at the corner.* **b.** to be introduced to. *How did you meet her?* **c.** to gather as a group or club. *Our dance class meets on Tuesdays.*

▶ **Meet** sounds like **meat**.

melt /mĕlt/ v. to change from solid form to liquid form by heating. *Ice becomes water when it melts.*

mile /mīl/ n. a measure of distance that is equal to 5,280 feet. *We drove two hundred miles on the first day of our trip.*

milk¹ /mĭlk/ n. a white drink that comes from cows or other animals. *I always drink milk with my lunch.*

milk² /mĭlk/ v. to get or draw milk from. *The farmer milks his cows twice a day.*

miss /mĭs/ v. (**miss•es, missed, miss•ing**) **a.** to fail to hit, reach, or get. *Her arrow missed the target by ten feet.* **b.** to feel sadness at the absence of someone or something. *We missed our dog while we were away.*

mon•key /mŭng' kē/ n. a small, long-tailed animal that lives in trees in the jungle. *Monkeys can swing from branch to branch.*

moo¹ /mo͞o/ n. the sound made by a cow. *The cow's moo was deep and loud.*

moo² /mo͞o/ v. to make this sound. *The cow mooed as I milked her.*

more /môr/ or /mōr/ adj. greater in number or amount. *You have more crayons than I do.*

moth /môth/ or /mŏth/ n. an insect that usually flies at night and is very much like a butterfly. *The moths fluttered around the porch light.*

much¹ /mŭch/ adj. (**more, most**) large in amount or degree. *We have so much homework to do!*

much² /mŭch/ n. a great amount. *I didn't get much at the store.*

mud /mŭd/ n. soft, wet, sticky dirt. *The car wheels got stuck in the mud.*

mule /myo͞ol/ n. a work animal that is part horse and part donkey. *Mules can carry heavy loads.*

mule

mumps /mŭmps/ n. a disease that causes swelling of the face and neck, making it hard to swallow. *We all got shots to prevent mumps.*

my /mī/ pron. of or belonging to me. *I'll meet you at my house.*

my•self /mī sĕlf'/ pron. (**our•selves** pl.) **a.** one's own self. *I guessed the answer by myself.* **b.** one's usual self. *When I was sick I didn't feel like myself.*

nail¹ /nāl/ n. a pointed piece of metal with a round or flat head. *We used a lot of nails on our tree house.*

nail² /nāl/ v. to fasten with nails. *The box was nailed shut.*

neat /nēt/ *adj.* clean; in order; tidy. *A neat store is a nice place to shop.*

need /nēd/ *v.* to require; to have to have. *Most plants need lots of sunshine to grow.*

new /nōō/ or /nyōō/ *adj.* **a.** just made or born; not old. *The new puppies can't leave their mother.* **b.** not the same as before. *We just moved to a new house.*

next /nĕkst/ *adj.* **a.** nearest; closest. *My best friend sat next to me.* **b.** just after; coming at once. *The next thing we will do is math.*

nice /nīs/ *adj.* (**nic•er, nic•est**) **a.** agreeable; pleasant. *Did you have a nice time at the picnic?* **b.** showing skill and care. *Kathy does a nice job of painting.*

nick•el /nĭk' əl/ *n.* **a.** a silver-gray metal. *Nickel is used in making magnets.* **b.** a coin worth five cents. *It takes twenty nickels to make one dollar.*

nine /nīn/ *n.* one more than eight; 9. *She said ten people would be there, but I only counted nine.*

nod /nŏd/ *v.* (**nods, nod•ded, nod•ding**) to bow the head and raise it quickly to say "yes" or "hello." *He nodded and waved to his friend.*

noon /nōōn/ *n.* the middle of the day; twelve o'clock in the daytime. *Our school serves lunch at noon.*

now /nou/ *adv.* at the time being talked about at present. *Carlos is opening the window now.*

Pronunciation Key

ă	pat	ŏ	pot	th	**th**in
ā	pay	ō	toe	*th*	**th**is
âr	care	ô	**paw, for**	hw	**wh**ich
ä	father	oi	n**oi**se	zh	vi**si**on
ĕ	pet	ou	**out**	ə	**a**bout,
ē	be	ŏŏ	t**oo**k		it**e**m,
ĭ	pit	ōō	b**oo**t		penc**i**l,
ī	pie	ŭ	c**u**t		gall**o**p,
îr	p**ier**	ûr	**ur**ge		circ**u**s

num • ber /nŭm' bər/ *n.* **a.** an amount; the total of persons or things. *What is the number of goats in that field?* **b.** a word or numeral that shows how many. *"Two" and "2" are both numbers.*

nurse /nûrs/ *n.* a person who cares for people who are sick or who need help. *Nurses work with doctors to help people stay well.*

nurse

off /ôf/ or /ŏf/ *adv.* **a.** away. *That hill is a long way off.* **b.** away from its present place. *Take your coat off.* **c.** not running; not on. *Please turn off the television.*

old /ōld/ *adj.* having lived or existed for a long time. *An old tree has a thick trunk.*

one /wŭn/ *n.* (**ones** *pl.*) **a.** the number that comes before two; 1. *I am the only one left.* **b.** a single person or thing. *She is the one we chose as our leader.*

or /ôr/ *conj.* a word used to express a choice or a difference. *Do you want soup or salad?*

our /our/ *pron.* of or belonging to us. *We ate our lunches outside.*

▶ **Our** sounds like **hour.**

out /out/ *adv.* away from the inside or center. *The cat ran out when we opened the door.*

out•side¹ /out sīd′/ *n.* the outer side. *Clean the outside of the windows.*

out•side² /out sīd′/ *adv.* outdoors. *Put the dog outside.*

own¹ /ōn/ *v.* to have; possess. *Who owns that blue car?*

own² /ōn/ *adj.* belonging to oneself. *Kate has her own room.*

pa•rade /pə rād′/ *n.* a march or procession. *We watched the circus parade.*

parade

park /pärk/ *n.* a piece of land where people can come to rest, play, or enjoy nature. *We saw a herd of deer in the park.*

part /pärt/ *n.* a piece or section; some; less than all. *Would you like part of my orange?*

pen•ny /pĕn′ ē/ *n.* (**pen•nies** *pl.*) a cent. *One hundred pennies make a dollar.*

pig•let /pĭg′ lĭt/ *n.* a young pig. *The piglets stayed in the pigpen.*

pink /pĭngk/ *n.* a pale reddish color. *That rose is a lovely shade of pink.*

pipe /pīp/ *n.* a long tube through which a liquid or gas may flow. *The pipes beneath the ground carry gas from Texas to Chicago.*

plant¹ /plănt/ *n.* a living thing that is not an animal. *Flowers, fruits, and vegetables are plants.*

plant² /plănt/ *v.* to put into the ground so that it will grow. *The farmer planted corn.*

play¹ /plā/ *v.* **a.** to take part in a game or activity for fun. *Children like to play tag.* **b.** to perform on a musical instrument. *I can play the piano.* **c.** to act on the stage. *Jennifer wants to play the queen.*

play² /plā/ *n.* a story written to be acted out. *The hero has the most lines in the play.*

please /plēz/ *v.* (**pleas•es, pleased, pleas•ing**) **a.** to give pleasure to; to bring happiness to. *My father's cooking pleases the family.* **b.** to be so kind as to. *Please help me.*

pond /pŏnd/ *n.* a little lake. *We can fish in the pond.*

prance /prăns/ *v.* (**pranc•es, pranced, pranc•ing**) to move in a lively or proud way. *The circus dogs pranced on their hind feet.*

put /po͝ot/ v. (**puts, put, put•ting**) to place; set. *I will put the plates on the table.*

puz•zle /pŭz′ əl/ n. a game with a problem to be worked out. *We do word puzzles in school.*

race¹ /rās/ n. a contest of speed. *During the summer we went to the boat races.*

race² /rās/ v. (**rac•es, raced, rac•ing**) to run or go fast. *The car raced down the road.*

rain¹ /rān/ n. drops of water that fall from clouds. *The rain splashed on the sidewalk.*

rain² /rān/ v. to fall in drops from the clouds. *Look how hard it is raining!*

rai•sin /rā′ zən/ n. a dried grape. *The pudding has raisins in it.*

rang /răng/ v. past tense of **ring**. *My alarm clock rang at seven.*

rash /răsh/ n. (**rash•es** pl.) small red spots that show up on the skin. *When I was sick I had an itchy rash.*

read /rēd/ v. (**reads, read, read•ing**) **a.** to get the meaning out of print or writing. *Do you like to read books?* **b.** to speak out loud something printed or written. *Please read your story to the class.*

red /rĕd/ n. the color of beets and most apples. *We saw a lot of red, white, and blue on July 4.*

rid•dle /rĭd′ l/ n. a puzzling problem; a question with a funny answer. *Can you solve this riddle?*

ring¹ /rĭng/ n. a metal circle worn on the finger as jewelry. *The stone in that ring is a diamond.*

ring

ring² /rĭng/ v. (**rings, rang, rung, ring•ing**) to make a clear sound. *Did the bell ring?*

road /rōd/ n. a way or path between places; highway. *This is the road to my friend's house.*

roar /rôr/ v. to make a loud, deep sound. *The lion roared and we all jumped.*

robe /rōb/ n. a long, loose garment. *After his shower he put on a robe.*

rock¹ /rŏk/ n. a hard mineral; a stone. *Can you skip a rock across the creek?*

rock² /rŏk/ v. to move back and forth. *I like to rock in a rocking chair.*

romp /rŏmp/ v. to play in a rough, lively way. *We watched the cubs romp.*

root¹ /ro͞ot/ or /ro͝ot/ n. the part of a plant that holds it in place and takes in food for it. *We eat some roots, such as carrots and beets.*

root² /ro͞ot/ v. to dig up. *The pigs rooted up the garden and made a mess.*

root³ /ro͞ot/ v. to support or cheer for. *We root for Mike's team.*

rub /rŭb/ v. (**rubs, rubbed, rub•bing**) to move back and forth against something. *The wheel of my bike rubs the fender.*

rush /rŭsh/ v. (**rush•es, rushed, rush•ing**) to move quickly, often with force. *The water rushed over the falls.*

sad /săd/ adj. (**sad•der, sad•dest**) unhappy. *We were sad when Jo left.*

safe /sāf/ adj. free from harm or danger. *We were safe in the house during the storm.*

said /sĕd/ v. past tense of **say**. *Su Li said she would come.*

sank /săngk/ v. past tense of **sink**. *The rock sank to the bottom of the stream.*

sat /săt/ v. past tense of **sit**. *We sat on the sofa.*

save /sāv/ v. (**saves, saved, sav•ing**) a. to rescue; to make safe from danger. *We saved the cat that was up in the tree.* b. to put away; keep. *I save stamps for my collection.*

saw¹ /sô/ n. a tool or machine used to cut. *Dad used his saw to build a birdhouse.*

saw² /sô/ v. past tense of **see**. *I saw the Big Dipper last night.*

say /sā/ v. (**says, said, say•ing**) a. to speak; put into words. *What did he say to you?* b. to give as an opinion. *I really can't say which I like best.*

scrub /skrŭb/ v. (**scrubs, scrubbed, scrub•bing**) to wash or clean by rubbing hard. *Doctors scrub their hands very carefully.*

sea /sē/ n. the ocean. *We walked on the beach by the sea.*

▶ **Sea** sounds like **see**.

seat /sēt/ n. a. a thing to sit on; a place to sit. *We do not have enough seats for the party.* b. the part of anything that is used for sitting. *Brian tore the seat of his pants.*

seat

sec•ond¹ /sĕk' ənd/ adj. next after the first. *We live in the second house from the corner.*

sec•ond² /sĕk' ənd/ n. a measure of time. *There are sixty seconds in a minute.*

see /sē/ v. (**sees, saw, seen, see•ing**) a. to look at; to be aware of by using the eyes. *I can see a truck on the road.* b. to find out. *See if she needs any help.* c. to understand. *Now I see how it works.*

▶ **See** sounds like **sea**.

seem /sēm/ v. to look like; to appear to be. *The new family next door seems very nice.*

seen /sēn/ v. a form of **see**. *Have you ever seen an elephant?*

send /sĕnd/ v. (**sends, sent, send•ing**) to cause or order to go. *Let's send a card to our teacher.*

sev • en /sev' ən/ n. the next number after six; six plus one; 7. *I added seven and three.*

shin /shĭn/ n. the front of the leg below the knee. *Fran scraped her shins during the soccer game.*

shine /shīn/ v. (**shines, shone** or **shined, shin•ing**) **a.** to give off light. *That light shines right in my eyes.* **b.** to make bright; to polish. *I helped my sister shine the pots and pans.*

shoe /shoo/ n. an outer cover for the foot. *My new shoes are waterproof.*

shoe

shore /shôr/ or /shōr/ n. the land at the edge of a lake, sea, or river. *We like to play in the sand at the shore.*

short /shôrt/ adj. **a.** not long or tall. *I look short next to my big brother.* **b.** not having enough. *When we passed out the worksheets, we were three short.* **c.** not having a long vowel sound. *The e in pet is a short vowel.*

shout /shout/ v. to call out loudly. *We shouted into the tunnel to hear the echo.*

Pronunciation Key

ă	pat	ŏ	pot	th	thin
ā	pay	ō	toe	th	this
âr	care	ô	paw, for	hw	which
ä	father	oi	noise	zh	vision
ĕ	pet	ou	out	ə	about,
ē	be	oo	took		item,
ĭ	pit	oo	boot		pencil,
ī	pie	ŭ	cut		gallop,
îr	pier	ûr	urge		circus

shrimp /shrĭmp/ n. (**shrimp** or **shrimps** pl.) a small shellfish with a long tail. *Shrimp taste good in salads.*

sick /sĭk/ adj. not well; having a disease. *Michelle stayed in bed when she was sick.*

si • lo /sī' lō/ n. a building, usually tall and round, for storing food for farm animals. *The silo stands next to the barn.*

sing /sĭng/ v. (**sings, sang, sung, sing•ing**) to make music with the voice. *Let's sing a round.*

sink¹ /sĭngk/ v. (**sinks, sank, sunk, sink•ing**) **a.** to go down. *The sun sinks in the west.* **b.** to make something go under. *That wave will sink the toy boat.*

sink² /sĭngk/ n. a kitchen or bathroom fixture. *He washed the dishes in the sink.*

sit /sĭt/ v. (**sits, sat, sit•ting**) **a.** to rest on the lower part of the body. *I will sit in this chair.* **b.** to settle; to rest. *Birds often sit on that branch.*

six /sĭks/ n. the next number after five; 6. *We need six on each team.*

Spelling Dictionary

six•ty /sĭks′ tē/ *n.* the next number after fifty-nine; 60. *Grandpa says he will retire at age sixty.*

skin /skĭn/ *n.* the outer layer of an animal's body or of some plants. *The apple had a red skin.*

sky /skī/ *n.* (**skies** *pl.*) the air high above the world; the space overhead. *Birds fly high in the sky.*

sleep¹ /slēp/ *n.* the resting of body and mind; the state of not being awake. *I had a good night's sleep.*

sleep² /slēp/ *v.* (**sleeps, slept, sleep•ing**) to be asleep; to rest the body and mind. *I am going to sleep over at Melanie's house tonight.*

slow¹ /slō/ *adj.* not moving fast or quickly. *The bus ride to school is so slow.*

slow² /slō/ *v.* to go slower. *A driver slows down and stops for a red light.*

small /smôl/ *adj.* **a.** not big; little. *A cub is a small bear.* **b.** not important. *We won't worry about that small detail.*

snack /snăk/ *n.* a small amount of food eaten between meals. *Fresh fruit makes a good snack.*

snail /snāl/ *n.* a slow-moving animal with a soft body and a shell. *The shell of a snail is carried on its back.*

sole /sōl/ *n.* the bottom of the foot. *The baby laughs when her sole is tickled.*

some /sŭm/ *adj.* **a.** a certain one, but not named or known. *Some girl called while you were out.* **b.** a number of. *Have some nuts.*

▶ **Some** sounds like **sum**.

spell /spĕl/ *v.* to put the letters of a word in the right order. *Some words are tricky to spell.*

spi•der /spī′ dər/ *n.* a small bug with eight long legs. *A spider spins a web to catch insects for its food.*

spot /spŏt/ *n.* a mark; a stain; a speck. *There are ink spots on this paper.*

sprout¹ /sprout/ *v.* to begin to grow. *The seeds are starting to sprout.*

sprout² /sprout/ *n.* a new growth. *There are some new sprouts on my plants.*

squeak /skwēk/ *n.* a sharp, high sound. *The squeaks of the mouse came from the cellar.*

star /stär/ *n.* **a.** a large body in space that we see as a small point of light on a clear night. *Our sun is a star that is close to the earth.* **b.** a shape with five or six points. *Our country's first flag had thirteen stars.*

star

stay /stā/ *v.* **a.** to remain. *Let's stay until four.* **b.** to keep on being. *It will stay cold all winter.*

stop /stŏp/ *v.* (**stops, stopped, stop•ping**) **a.** to prevent. *We want to stop crime.* **b.** to come to a halt. *Why did that car stop out front?*

store /stôr/ or /stōr/ *n.* a place where things are sold. *Salim bought a hammer in the hardware store.*

stripe /strīp/ *n.* a long narrow strip or band of a different color. *Tigers and zebras have stripes.*

such /sŭch/ *adj.* **a.** so much; so great. *The game was such fun that we hated to stop.* **b.** of a certain kind. *Good ball players such as José are hard to find.*

sum /sŭm/ *n.* the number made by adding numbers. *The sum of 7 and 3 is 10.*

▶ **Sum** sounds like **some**.

swamp /swŏmp/ *n.* a soft, very wet piece of land. *Moss hangs from the trees in some swamps.*

tad•pole /tăd′ pōl′/ *n.* a very young frog that still lives underwater and has gills and a long tail. *Tadpoles grow legs while they live in water.*

tail /tāl/ *n.* the part of an animal's body at the end of its backbone, especially a growth that sticks out beyond the body. *My dog has a bushy tail.*

tail

▶ **Tail** sounds like **tale**.

Pronunciation Key

ă	pat	ŏ	pot	th	thin
ā	pay	ō	toe	th	this
âr	care	ô	paw, for	hw	which
ä	father	oi	noise	zh	vision
ĕ	pet	ou	out	ə	about,
ē	be	ŏŏ	took		item,
ĭ	pit	ōō	boot		pencil,
ī	pie	ŭ	cut		gallop,
îr	pier	ûr	urge		circus

take /tāk/ *v.* (**takes, took, tak•en, tak•ing**) **a.** to grip; to hold on to. *Take my hand when we cross the street.* **b.** to carry. *Can anyone take this box to the office?*

tale /tāl/ *n.* a story. *The teacher told us a tale about a talking turtle.*

▶ **Tale** sounds like **tail**.

talk /tôk/ *v.* to speak; to say words. *Can the baby talk yet?*

tall /tôl/ *adj.* **a.** high; not short. *There are many tall trees in the forest.* **b.** being a stated height. *My brother is five feet tall.*

tall tale /tôl′ tāl′/ *n.* a story that is hard to believe, often one handed down through the years. *I think tall tales about pioneer days are exciting.*

tape /tāp/ *n.* a narrow strip or band of cloth, plastic, etc. *The doctor put tape around my sore ankle.*

team /tēm/ *n.* a group of people working, acting, or playing together. *Are you on the baseball team?*

tear /târ/ *v.* (**tears, tore, torn, tear•ing**) **a.** to rip or pull apart. *How did you tear your shirt?* **b.** to pull with force. *Did she tear the picture?*

teeth /tēth/ *n. pl.* more than one tooth. *Did you brush your teeth this morning?*

teeth

tell /tĕl/ *v.* (tells, told, tell•ing) **a.** to say; to talk about. *Tell us a story.* **b.** to make known. *Don't tell the answer to anyone.*

ten /tĕn/ *n.* one more than nine; 10. *Ten is a nice round number.*

than /thăn/ or /thən/ *conj.* compared to or with. *Kim is taller than Janet.*

thank /thăngk/ *v.* to say or show you are pleased and grateful. *I want to thank Grandfather for my game.*

that¹ /thăt/ or /thət/ *pron.* the person or thing pointed out. *Take that to school today.*

that² /thăt/ or /thət/ *adj.* being the one farther away. *Give that boy a pencil.*

thaw /thô/ *v.* to melt. *The ice thawed in the spring.*

them /thĕm/ *pron.* the ones spoken about. *We saw them working on the house.*

these /thēz/ *pron., adj.* plural of **this**. *Give me three of these flowers.*

they /thā/ *pron.* the ones spoken about. *Liz and Dennis said they would come.*

third¹ /thûrd/ *n.* one of three equal parts. *Each of us three did a third of the work.*

third² /thûrd/ *adj.* next after the second. *That was the third yellow car we've seen.*

thir•ty /thûr' tē/ *n.* one more than twenty-nine; 30. *He started college when he was thirty.*

this¹ /thĭs/ *pron.* the thing or person nearby or spoken of just before. *This is my cat.*

this² /thĭs/ *adj.* being the one nearby. *This plant blooms, but that one does not.*

those /thōz/ *pron., adj.* plural of **that**. *Those are the ones we need.*

three /thrē/ *n.* one more than two; 3. *Jon took two books and Dan took three.*

throat /thrōt/ *n.* the passage between the mouth and the stomach and lungs. *She stayed home because she had a sore throat.*

ti•ger /tī' gər/ *n.* a large cat with yellowish fur and black stripes. *Tigers live in Asia.*

toad /tōd/ *n.* an animal much like a frog, with rough, brown skin. *Toads live on land and eat bugs.*

toe /tō/ *n.* one of the five end parts of the front of the foot. *Rita wiggled her toes in the mud.*

toe•nail /tō' nāl'/ *n.* the hard, thin layer at the end of each toe. *I must cut my toenails tonight.*

told /tōld/ *v.* past tense of **tell**. *I told him how to get there.*

too /tōō/ *adv.* **a.** also; in addition. *If you go to the game, we will go, too.* **b.** more than enough. *The sheet is too big for the bed.*

▶ **Too** sounds like **two**.

took /tŏŏk/ *v.* past tense of **take**. *Mom took us fishing.*

tool /tōōl/ *n.* something held in the hand and used to do work. *Hammers and saws are tools.*

tooth /tōōth/ *n.* (**teeth** *pl.*) one of the hard, bonelike parts in the jaw used for chewing. *The dentist filled a cavity in my tooth.*

torn /tôrn/ *v.* a form of **tear**. *Angie had torn her skirt.*

town /toun/ *n.* a community larger than a village but smaller than a city. *The people in our town are proud of it.*

train /trān/ *n.* a line of connected railroad or subway cars. *Many people take a train to work every day.*

train

trash /trăsh/ *n.* something that is no longer valuable; a useless thing; rubbish. *These old toys are trash; throw them out.*

tree /trē/ *n.* a large plant having a woody trunk with branches and leaves at its upper part. *Forests are made up of many trees.*

try /trī/ *v.* (**tries, tried, try•ing**) to attempt. *Try to answer all of the questions.*

twen•ty /twĕn′ tē/ *n.* one more than nineteen; 20. *Josh thought twenty was too many birthday guests.*

Pronunciation Key

ă	pat	ŏ	pot	th	**th**in
ā	pay	ō	toe	th	**th**is
âr	care	ô	paw, for	hw	**wh**ich
ä	father	oi	noise	zh	vi**s**ion
ĕ	pet	ou	out	ə	**a**bout,
ē	be	ŏŏ	took		item,
ĭ	pit	ōō	boot		penc**i**l,
ī	pie	ŭ	cut		gall**o**p,
îr	pier	ûr	urge		circ**u**s

two /tōō/ *n.* one more than one; 2. *Two plus two is four.*

▶ **Two** sounds like **too**.

wait /wāt/ *v.* to stay or stop until something happens or someone comes. *Wait for me at the park.*

walk /wôk/ *v.* to go on foot at a normal rate. *We walk to school every day.*

wall /wôl/ *n.* the side of a room, house, or other building. *That wall has no windows in it.*

want /wŏnt/ or /wônt/ *v.* to wish for. *I want a new coat.*

wash /wŏsh/ or /wôsh/ *v.* (**wash•es, washed, wash•ing**) to clean with water or another liquid. *He will wash the dishes for us.*

wave /wāv/ *n.* **a.** a high ridge that moves across the surface of a body of water. *Waves make the ocean exciting.* **b.** the moving of the hand in greeting. *She gave a wave as she passed us.*

Spelling Dictionary

weave /wēv/ v. (**weaves, wove** or **weaved, wo•ven, weav•ing**) to make by lacing threads under and over each other. *She is weaving yarn into cloth.*

web /wĕb/ n. anything that has been woven. *Spiders catch flies in their webs.*

web

week /wēk/ n. a period of seven days, especially from Sunday to Saturday. *This is the third week of the month.*

well¹ /wĕl/ n. a hole dug in the ground to get water, oil, or gas. *The water from our well is good and cold.*

well² /wĕl/ adv. (**bet•ter, best**) in a good or pleasing way; with skill. *He did the job well.*

went /wĕnt/ v. past tense of **go**. *We went downtown.*

what /hwŏt/ pron. **a.** which thing or things. *What did you forget?* **b.** that which; the thing that. *I know what you mean.*

wheat /hwēt/ n. a kind of grass that bears a grain. *Flour is made by grinding wheat.*

when¹ /hwĕn/ adv. at what time. *When may we go?*

when² /hwĕn/ conj. after. *You may go when the work is done.*

which /hwĭch/ pron. what one. *Which of those boys is your friend?*

while¹ /hwīl/ n. a length of time. *Can you wait a while for my answer?*

while² /hwīl/ conj. during the time that. *Come and see our house while you are here.*

white /hwīt/ n. the color of snow. *White is the absence of color.*

who /hoo/ pron. **a.** what person or persons. *Who gave you that book?* **b.** that. *The person who asked for the book is not here.*

why¹ /hwī/ adv. for what reason. *Why did you come to see me?*

why² /hwī/ conj. the reason for which. *I know why Adam left.*

will /wĭl/ v. (**would**) am, is or are going to. *We will see you next week.*

win /wĭn/ v. (**wins, won, win•ning**) **a.** to gain a victory. *Do you think our team can win?* **b.** to get or earn. *Nina's pig may win a ribbon at the fair.*

wind /wĭnd/ n. air that is moving. *The wind is from the north.*

wing /wĭng/ n. the part of a bird or insect that keeps and moves it in the air. *A hawk can spread its wings and glide.*

wink /wĭngk/ v. to close and open one eye quickly as a kind of signal. *Aunt Emily winked at me behind Mom's back.*

win • ner /wĭn′ ər/ *n.* a person, thing, or group that wins. *Maria's poem was the winner in the writing contest.*

wish[1] /wĭsh/ *v.* (**wish•es, wished, wish•ing**) to want; to have a desire for. *I wish he could come.*

wish[2] /wĭsh/ *n.* (**wish•es** *pl.*) something wanted. *Did your wish come true?*

won /wŭn/ *v.* past tense of **win**. *Which team won?*

wood /wŏŏd/ *n.* the hard inside part of a tree, beneath its bark. *Oak and walnut are hard woods.*

wool /wŏŏl/ *n.* **a.** the soft, curly hair of a sheep. *Wool is shaved from sheep in the spring.* **b.** the yarn or cloth made from the hair of a sheep. *In winter he wore a cap of wool.*

Pronunciation Key

ă	pat	ŏ	pot	th	**th**in
ā	pay	ō	toe	*th*	**th**is
âr	care	ô	paw, for	hw	**wh**ich
ä	father	oi	noise	zh	vision
ĕ	pet	ou	**ou**t	ə	**a**bout,
ē	be	ŏŏ	took		item,
ĭ	pit	ōō	boot		pencil,
ī	pie	ŭ	cut		gallop,
îr	pier	ûr	urge		circus

yarn /yärn/ *n.* wool or other spun fiber used in needlework. *My aunt bought balls of red yarn to make me a sweater for my birthday.*

yarn

yel • low /yĕl′ ō/ *n.* the color of a lemon or of butter. *Yellow is a bright, sunny color.*

yard[1] /yärd/ *n.* a measure of length. *One yard is the same as three feet or thirty-six inches.*

yard[2] /yärd/ *n.* the open ground around a house, school, or other building. *Children were playing in the yard.*